Stewards of Access
Custodians of Choice

A Philosophical Foundation
for Parks, Recreation, and Tourism

Fourth Edition

Daniel Dustin   **Leo McAvoy**   **John Schultz**
Kelly Bricker   **Jeff Rose**   **Keri Schwab**

SAGAMORE
PUBLISHING

©2011 Sagamore Publishing LLC
All Rights Reserved.

Publishers: Joseph J. Bannon, Peter L. Bannon
Director of Sales and Marketing: M. Douglas Sanders
Director of Development and Production: Susan M. Davis
Pen and Ink Drawings: Kathleen Dustin

ISBN print edition: 978-1-57167-658-0
ISBN ebook: 978-1-57167-659-7
Library of Congress Catalog Card Number:2010942516

Printed in the United States.

Sagamore Publishing LLC
1807 N Federal Dr.
Urbana, IL 61801
www.sagamorepub.com

To John Schultz
mentor, colleague, and friend

> " *All things living* and all things not living are the products of the same primal explosion and evolutionary history and hence are interrelated in an internal way from the very beginning. We are distant cousins to the stars and near relations to the oceans, plants, and all other living creatures on our planet. "
>
> —Sally McFague

Contents

Part I

The Sacred Tree Is Dead

Part II

Emergence of a Worth Ethic

Part III

Pathways to the Future

Epilogue

Preface to the Fourth Edition

We thank Sagamore Publishing LLC for making this fourth edition of *Stewards of Access/Custodians of Choice* possible. Almost 30 years have passed since we penned the first edition, and we are happy to report that our fundamental convictions about the importance of parks, recreation, and tourism to enhancing the quality of life remain unchanged. At the same time, we recognize that while our convictions remain unchanged, the world has changed dramatically in the last three decades. Overpopulation, resource depletion, climate change, and a host of other pressing social and environmental problems challenge us to demonstrate the relevance of parks, recreation, and tourism to their resolution. To that end, we continue to believe in the profession's instrumental value and that a healthy environment is the foundation upon which humankind's long-term welfare ultimately depends.

It is our pleasure to welcome three new co-authors to this fourth edition: Kelly Bricker, Jeff Rose, and Keri Schwab. Kelly specializes in ecotourism, biodiversity health, and sustainability. Jeff specializes in human-environment relationships and matters of social and environmental justice. Keri specializes in family leisure, mothers' leisure, and youth development. Kelly, Jeff, and Keri have expanded our understanding of the world, and this edition's closing chapters reflect that expanded understanding. It is a privilege and a joy to add our voices to the conversation about the role of parks, recreation, and tourism in contemporary life, and we look forward to hearing more of Kelly, Jeff, and Keri's voices in the future.

We added two chapters to the Epilogue, reflecting our growing belief that health promotion within the context of social and environmental justice is the profession's destiny. Chapter 13, "People and Nature: Toward an Ecological Model of Health Promotion," is reprinted with permission from *Leisure Sciences*. It illustrates the relationship between human health and biodiversity health and underscores why the health of the biosphere is critical to the health of humankind. Chapter 14, "Ecological Democracy: Cultivating Healthy Citizens," considers what we are obliged to do with our health as citizens in a participatory democracy. It is a call for civic engagement and a challenge to each and every one of us to employ our individual skills and abilities in service of the public good.

We also reworked some of our language from previous editions, updated references, and wrote several new discussion questions. Most notably, we added tourism to parks and recreation when referring to the profession as a whole to honor its growth and development. While we recognize the limitations of labeling (see Chapter 8), we chose not to create a "laundry list" of a title to describe the profession. We implore readers to think of parks, recreation, and tourism as broadly conceived and recognize that the profession is made up of an amalgam of specializations, all of which are united by a common interest in serving the human potential. We have tried to write in a way that respects multiple interpretations of the human experience while standing by our fundamental convictions. Finally, we acknowledge our positionality as three privileged white males who, in the twilight of our careers, remain committed to our own continuing education.

Daniel Dustin
Leo McAvoy
John Schultz

Introduction

"The falcon cannot hear the falconer;
Things fall apart; the center cannot hold."

—William Butler Yeats

". . . During the Middle Ages, cathedrals were built by [the] voluntary labor of thousands of people. There is an old story about three such workers. They were stone cutters. A fourth man asked each one, in turn, the same question, 'What are you doing?'

The first answered, 'I'm cutting stone.'

The second said, 'I'm building a cathedral.'

The third smiled and answered quietly, 'I'm glorifying God.'" [1]

This book is the product of six individuals who view the park, recreation, and tourism profession from a perspective not unlike that of the third stone cutter. The purpose of the book is to share that perspective with you. If you are of the ilk of the first or second stone cutter, we hope the book will elevate you to the third perspective. If, on the other hand, you are already there, the book may still serve as your companion and comfort you with the knowledge that you are not alone in your thinking.

This work has evolved out of our concern for the future of parks, recreation, and tourism. While there is broad agreement within the profession regarding the importance of its services to the well-being of America's citizenry, it has been difficult to rally support for those services from the citizenry itself. Efforts to gain recognition and acceptance as a vital area of human service by the profession's subgroups have led to factionalism and frustration. As Bruno Geba noted, "different groups are pulling in many directions, and basic principles of recreation are being replaced to fit the needs of others.

The profession, as a result, is ripped into pieces, leaving its members without a unifying core."[2]

The task of this book is to reconstruct that unifying core of principles and practices that collectively define the unique contribution of parks, recreation, and tourism to the quality of life. Borrowing from E. F. Schumacher, "it is not as if we had to invent anything new; at the same time, it is not good enough merely to revert to the old formulations. Our task ... is to understand the present world, the world in which we live, and make our choices." [3]

To that end, the book has three objectives. First, it is a study of recreational conduct, both in terms of the individual and in terms of those responsible for planning, managing, and evaluating park, recreation, and tourism services. Second, it is a statement of philosophy, a reconciliation of the recreational needs of people with a concern for the social and natural environment in which those needs are expressed. Third, it is an excursion into the future, an application of the philosophical foundation established in the second part of the book to issues that will shape the park, recreation, and tourism profession in years to come.

In accordance with its three objectives, the book is divided into three parts. Each part is guided by a selected passage from Jacob Bronowski's book *Science and Human Values*. [4] Part I, "The Sacred Tree is Dead," evolves from the following passage:

> If we are to study conduct, we must follow it both directions: into the duties of [people], which alone hold a society together, and also into the freedom to act personally which the society must still allow its [people]. The problem of values arises only when [people] try to fit together their need to be social animals with their need to be free [people]. There is no problem and there are no values, until [people] want to do both.

Part II, "Emergence of a Work Ethic," evolves from the following passage:

> The concepts of value are profound and difficult exactly because they do two things at once: they join [people] into societies, and

yet they preserve for them a freedom which makes them single [individuals]. A philosophy which does not acknowledge both needs cannot evolve values, and indeed cannot allow them.

Part III, "Pathways to the Future," evolves from the following passage:

> [We] master nature not by force but by understanding ... we have learned that we gain our ends only with the laws of nature; we control [nature] only by understanding [its] laws ... we must be content that power is the byproduct of understanding.

In essence, this book is an application of Bronowski's thinking to the park, recreation, and tourism profession; first, as it relates to understanding recreational conduct in the United States; second, as it relates to a worth ethic as a philosophical foundation for parks, recreation, and tourism; and third, as it relates to the relevance of a worth ethic to issues of growing importance within the profession.

That application process is the stuff out of which this book is made. Such a connective or synthesizing approach to the problems confronting our field represents a departure from the more traditional academic approach described by Aldo Leopold:

> There are [people] charged with the duty of examining the construction of plants, animals, and soils which are the instruments of the great orchestra. These [people] are called professors. Each selects one instrument and spends his [or her] life taking it apart and describing its strings and sounding boards. ... [Professors] may pluck the strings of [their] own instruments, but never that of another, and if [they] listen for music [they] must never admit it to [their] fellows or to [their] students. For all are restrained by an ironbound taboo which decrees that the construction of instruments is the domain of science, while the detection of harmony is the domain of poets. [5]

While we do not claim to be poets, throughout our writing we have been conscious of Leopold's words. Consequently, while we have undoubtedly lapsed into professorial habits from time to time, we have tried to communicate in a way that reflects one ear bent to the music.

As a final note, although it may seem presumptuous for six educators to attempt to speak for the entire park, recreation, and tourism profession, we have been compelled to do so based on the conviction that the profession urgently needs to articulate its reason for being to the American public in such a way that they will insist on its continued service. In the absence of a convincing purpose statement, it is likely that the profession will remain vulnerable to attack from both within and without its ranks. Under the circumstances, if it is to survive, even a turtle has to stick its neck out from time to time. [6]

So this book begins. It is testimony to the value of the park, recreation, and tourism profession and those who serve it—the stewards of access, the custodians of choice.

Part I

THE SACRED TREE IS DEAD

" If we are to study conduct, we must follow it both directions: into the duties of [people], which alone hold a society together, and also into the freedom to act personally which the society must still allow its [people]. The problem of values arises only when [people] try to fit together their need to be social animals with their need to be free [people]. There is no problem and there are no values, until [people] want to do both. "

—**Jacob Bronowski**

1

The Problem

"The earth, like the sun, like the air,
belongs to everyone—and to no one."

—Edward Abbey

On the western slope of California's Sierra Nevada stands the largest living thing on Earth. The General Sherman Tree, known formally as *Sequoia gigantea,* is monumental both in its size and in its effect on those who visit it. The great tree has a diameter of more than 30 feet at the base. Rising skyward to a height of 120 feet, its trunk is still 17 feet thick. Nearly 130 feet from the ground, the first large limb is almost seven feet in diameter. Finally, 272 feet above the forest floor, is the top of its crown.

Standing beneath this giant sequoia, one is struck by its seemingly impregnable nature. Other trees are taller than the General Sherman, but none matches its volume. Moreover, its 1,385 tons bear down heavily on the observer. It is, in the words of Freeman Tilden, a "prodigious club." [1] Having withstood the test of time (more than 2,500 years), the General Sherman Tree is a symbol of strength and security, a living fortress unto the ages.

How puzzling, then, that a young National Park Service naturalist should be toting bag after bag of ground cover to the base of this monarch. She explains that the root system of a giant sequoia penetrates only six feet into the earth, and that almost two feet of that soil have been worn away by the footsteps of admiring recreationists. Wanting to be photographed by the General Sherman Tree, to touch it, perhaps for a moment even to be fused with its greatness, well-meaning people inadvertently have removed one third of the big tree's foundation.

How has this point in American history been reached where even the most durable of the nation's recreation resources are in jeopardy from an admiring, touching, and loving public? By what right do Americans claim access to these resources? Having achieved it, what explains the nature of their recreational conduct? How have park, recreation, and tourism professionals traditionally responded to the public's recreational demands? By what logic have we carried out our responsibilities? And what, if anything, should we do differently in the future?

These questions, considered collectively, constitute the problem of this book. Through their probing and discussion in Part I, the necessary groundwork is laid down upon which to base the philosophical statement made in Part II. We encourage you to read this first section carefully. Our philosophical foundation for the park, recreation, and tourism profession rests on it.

Past as Prologue

In his book *America as a Civilization*, Max Lerner stated that "the most important fact about a people is the life force carried along from its cultural origins," which is "crossed, blended, and transmuted with others in a developing civilization." [2] To understand the nature of recreational conduct in the United States today, it is therefore necessary to know something of the life force that defines the American character. And to gain that knowledge, it is necessary to look backward in time.

"The people who came to the American shores felt intensely about the American experience, because for each of them America was the wall broken down, door broken open ... whether they came for land or economic opportunity or freedom, they came because of the past denials in their lives." [3] As the national character unfurled, "it was free enterprise arrayed against mercantilism, laissez faire against cameralism, individualism against hierarchy, natural rights against monarchy, popular nationalism against the dynastic regimes, social mobility against caste, the pioneering spirit against the status quo." [4] It was the crossing, blending, and transmuting, then, of the values embedded in free enterprise, laissez faire, individualism, natural rights, popular nationalism, social mobility, and the pioneering spirit that helped shape the contemporary American life force. But it was also more than this.

In his reflective work *Democracy in America,* nineteenth century Frenchman Alexis de Tocqueville addressed the passion with which democratic people pursued "equality of condition." [5] Noting the particular strength of that passion following the overthrow of oppressive social systems, Tocqueville reasoned that at such times people "pounce upon equality as their booty, and they cling to it as to some precious treasure which they fear to lose." [6] So it was that the American people, imbued with confidence in their ability to create their own destiny, and encouraged to do so by their newly won equality of condition, blazed a trail of self-determination across the North American continent.

Fueling the drive westward was the logic contained in Adam Smith's *Wealth of Nations.* [7] Believing that individuals were the best judges of their own welfare, and that people who looked after their own interests would be led by an "invisible hand" to promote the public interest, America's developers felt sanctified in their individual pursuits. Commenting on this trait, Tocqueville observed that democratic communities are constantly filled with people "who, having entered but yesterday upon their independent condition, are intoxicated with their new power. They entertain a presumptuous confidence in their own strength, and as they do not suppose that they can henceforward ever have occasion to claim the assistance of their fellow creatures, they do not scruple to show that they care for nobody but themselves." [8]

Perhaps the clearest expression of the tenacity with which early Americans embraced the ideals of Adam Smith was in their settlement of the western frontier. The homesteading of public land for private profit was promoted for its indirect benefits to the developing nation as well as its direct rewards to the individual homesteader. In a country of inexhaustible resources, the guidance of the "invisible hand" went unquestioned. Moreover, it contributed significantly to the increasing realization of what is known to this day as the American dream—the ownership of property. "Men of small property," Tocqueville called them, "a class that is constantly increased by the equality of conditions." [9] Americans coveted property. Americans collected property. Americans championed property rights. They were indeed making up for past denials in their lives.

The picture is now painted of a democratic nation peopled with confident individualists who, having earned independence and equality of condition, exercised their pioneering spirit in the form of free enterprise and laissez faire. Mentally equipped with Adam Smith's economic rationale for asserting their natural rights to the nation's common stock of resources, they boldly set out to better their position through the acquisition of property. This was, and largely continues to be, the driving life force of the American people.

Parks are for People

How has this life force expressed itself in the recreational conduct of the American public? In his book *The National Park Service*, William Everhart credits Tocqueville with predicting that in America many would demand what in other lands had been reserved for the few. [10] Everhart adds that "parks, whether national, state, or municipal, are one of the best expressions of this ideal. [11] From Yosemite to the Boston Common, recreation resources represent the democratic principle of the public good. They belong to all Americans.

There is a symbolic significance to public recreation areas that transcends their everyday meaning. In a nation committed to equality of conditions, public parks and playgrounds serve an equalizing function. Regardless of one's station in life, one has the right of access to these resources. They are both the poor person's and the rich person's property. [12, 13]

Only in recent years, however, have significant numbers of Americans expressed their right of access to public recreation areas. Previously they had been busy with other things. As Foster Dulles notes in *A History of Recreation: America Learns to Play*, prior to the twentieth century "our only pleasure was business, our only amusement making money." [14] American history had revolved around hard work and productivity. But now it was time to enjoy the fruits of those labors. An increasing equality of conditions, characterized by more time, more money, more education, and more mobility, made it possible for millions of Americans to get acquainted with their recreational properties.

Accompanying the skyrocketing demand for recreation opportunities was a distinctive character to the recreational conduct itself. The acquisitive nature of the American people, which had been manifested historically in the collection of property, was now manifested in the collection of experiences. Recreationists were more interested in intensiveness of consumption than intensiveness of experience. [15] Consequently, their conduct was marked by an indulgent quality. Again the words of Tocqueville, written so long ago, are prophetic. "He who has set his heart exclusively upon the pursuit of worldly welfare is always in a hurry, for he has but a limited time at his disposal to reach, grasp, and to enjoy it. The recollection of the shortness of life is a constant spur to him. Besides the good things that he possesses, he every instant fancies a thousand others that death will prevent him from trying if he does not try them soon." [16] Anxious to express their right of access, to claim their fair share of the nation's public recreational goods, Americans thus began to recreate in increasing numbers—while there was still time.

In their collective haste, the citizenry demanded freedom of recreational action as well. Since public recreation areas belong to all Americans, it was reasoned that everyone had a right to behave as they wished when frequenting their properties. Recreational preferences were viewed purely as matters of private taste. [17] And the essence of the recreation experience itself was understood to hinge on freedom of choice. It was a line of thought quite consistent with that of Adam Smith.

The picture now emerges of a democratic nation peopled with confident recreationists who, having earned access through an expanding equality of conditions, exercise their recreational preferences in an acquisitive and individualistic manner. Bolstered yet by Adam Smith's philosophical rationale for asserting their natural rights to the nation's common pool of resources, they boldly set out to enjoy themselves. Paraphrasing Dulles, the democracy finally came into its recreational heritage. [18]

Problems in the Parks

While the arrival of recreation in America as a popular human pastime is certainly cause for celebration, it brings with it a new set of problems for the stewards and custodians of recreation areas and facilities—problems related to increasing demands on limited resources. Moreover, they are particularly thorny problems because they are bound up inextricably with what has been described already as the contemporary American life force.

To get at the root of these problems, it is again instructive to turn to Lerner. He argues that there is no single key to unlocking American civilization. Rather, it is necessary to focus on the inter-relationships and interactions among the various elements of the American life force in the search for understanding. [19] So to get at the crux of the difficulty described above—increasing demands on limited resources—it is necessary to focus on the interrelationships and interactions between, what Lerner calls, "economic man and psychological man—the materialist emphasis and the individualist emphasis." [20]

The American appetite for material goods has been discussed already in the context of love of property. Of interest now is the insatiable nature of that appetite. Almost 150 years ago, Tocqueville pictured Americans as "forever brooding over advantages they do not possess." [21] More recently, Philip Slater, upon returning to the United States from a visit to an impoverished Third World country, reflected that "it is difficult to become reaccustomed to seeing people already weighted down with possessions acting as if every object they did not own were bread withheld from a hungry mouth."[22]

Indeed it is difficult to understand a people who, by any standard other than their own, are well off behave as if they were continually starving for material goods. What is it that makes Americans always want more?

The answer, not surprisingly, is embedded in the psychology of American history. In a country of equalizing social conditions, the accumulation of material wealth was a way of distinguishing oneself, a way of elevating one's social status. Conspicuous consumption thus became a driving force in the continuing motivation of the American consumer. [23] Coupled with a market economy that was well suited to stimulate and generate tastes and desires, [24] the allure of conspicuous consumption created a social climate in which Americans were led to believe they never possessed quite enough of anything. It is a cultural characteristic that flourishes to this day. [25]

As Lerner points out, however, materialism by itself does not explain the increasing demands placed on the nation's common store of resources. It is the interrelationship and interaction between materialism and individualism that accounts for such demands. While materialism provides the incentive for resource exploitation, individualism provides the license. Employing the logic of Adam Smith, Americans claim access to public resources because they are confident that private use will result ultimately in public gain. The philosophy of the "invisible hand" guarantees it.

But here's the rub. While Adam Smith's thinking provided a justifiable rationale for expansion and growth during America's formative years, its continued influence is having a dramatically different effect in an era of limits. As E. F. Schumacher argued, "an attitude to life which seeks fulfillment in the single-minded pursuit of wealth—in short, materialism—does not fit into this world, because it contains within itself no limiting principle, while the environment in which it is placed is strictly limited." [26]

It is the resultant collision between a highly materialistic and individualistic America and a limited resource base that constitutes one of the major problems facing American civilization today. It is a problem that has been outlined vividly in its recreational context by Joseph Sax in *Mountains without Handrails*:

> Recreation that is dependent on ever-increasing growth and impact for its satisfactions is insatiable. The scarcity of resources we encounter in trying to meet such recreational demand is as much a psychological as a physical problem. No matter how much land we have, more will always be demanded because the object is itself more, more of whatever there is. This is what the Spanish philosopher José Ortega y Gasset called 'the psychology of the spoiled child' who is insatiable because his object is not some particular thing, but a larger share. Increase is itself the object of his desire.[27]

Unfortunately, in a world of limits, such insatiable desires lead in but one direction.

Tragedy of the Commons

That direction has been mapped thoroughly by Garrett Hardin in "The Tragedy of the Commons." [28] Published in 1968, Hardin's essay traces the consequences of a philosophy of unlimited access to commonly held resources for both human beings and the environment of which they are a part. It is a path, Hardin contends, of mutual destruction.

Although Hardin makes his argument in the context of the world population problem, his logic can be extended to an entire class of problems characterized by increasing demands on limited resources. It is important, therefore, for park, recreation, and tourism professionals who are now confronted with a problem of this kind to understand the point of view expressed in that essay.

To illustrate the tragedy of the commons, Hardin asks us to imagine a pasture, fixed in size, which is accessible to all the residents of a village. Each villager, being rational, wants to maximize his or her use of the pasture by grazing as many cattle as possible. Therefore, the villagers continually expand the size of their respective herds, recognizing that the benefits from such expansion will be theirs alone, while any costs associated with the increased grazing will be shared among all the village members. Under these circumstances, expansion only seems sensible. What each villager fails to recognize, however, is that every other villager is following the same logic, and that the cumulative effect of their independently logical action is bound to be the destruction of the pasture. Blinded by self-interest, the villagers proceed in their unremitting exploitation of the commonly held resource. Therein lies the tragedy. [29]

According to Hardin, there are no technical solutions to problems of this kind. For example, the technical solutions likely to be applied in the above situation are irrigation and fertilization of the land to increase its productivity. Such measures can provide only intermediate relief, however, if the villagers continue to add to their numbers of cattle. Without a fundamental change in their attitude toward the pasture, they will conduct business as usual, resulting in the pasture's eventual despoliation. Clearly, given increasing demand for a finite resource, technical solutions will prove inadequate in the long run.

Hardin argues that the only permanent solution must stem from a basic change in human values. In the above situation, the only permanent solution to the problem of overuse of the pasture must stem from a fundamental change in the way the villagers treat it. While it is widely assumed that such value change comes through education, Hardin contends that education alone will not result in the desired change. Knowledge about the dangers of overgrazing will tend to be heeded only by the conscientious villagers, leaving those who are less conscientious even more incentive to pursue their self-interests. The only realistic solution to this problem, Hardin maintains, is that of "mutually agreed upon coercion." [30] That is, those people who are affected by the use of the pasture must agree to a method of coercion that will limit its use. Such coercion might take the form of a graduated tax on the profits derived from the sale of the cattle. Or it might take the form of a law setting a limit on the number of animals each villager may graze on the pasture. Regardless of the method employed, the point is that such coercive measures require a new set of values which are based on the realization that technical solutions and educational processes by themselves are inadequate in resolving problems associated with unlimited use of a common resource. Such a value system would justify coercive methods, therefore, by the knowledge that without them "freedom in a commons brings ruin to all." [31]

Tragedy of the Recreation Commons

The tragedy of the commons denotes a situation where a group of individuals, each acting in their own individual best interest, find that the collective effect of their independently logical action is actually negative. Consider, for example, an urban resident who wishes to escape the heat, congestion, and noise of the city on a summer weekend. She looks to the mountains (beach, lake, river, countryside) for a cool, quiet, and refreshing two-day respite. She gathers the family, packs the car, and heads for one of America's nearby public recreation areas. It's a logical thing to do. But consider also the implication of thousands upon thousands of similar city dwellers who are making the same independently logical decision. The cumulative effect of such numbers of people seeking a cool, quiet, and refreshing recreational experience at the same time is one of destroying the very values for which they are searching. Instead of peace and relaxation in the out-of-doors, they are treated to traffic jams, congestion, and noise—the very problems from which they are trying to escape. It is a vivid example of the tragedy of the commons.

This time the commons is a recreation setting, and the tragedy is allowed to occur because park, recreation, and tourism professionals are reluctant to exclude anyone from visiting what lawfully belongs to everyone. We are fully aware, after all, of the democratic principle of the public good. But as recreational demands mount—and mount they will in Adam Smith's America—the direction toward which a philosophy of unlimited access inevitably leads is one of continually eroding quality in both recreation opportunities and environments. 32 In that respect, freedom in a recreation commons may indeed bring ruin to all—even, Hardin would hasten to add, to the largest living thing on Earth.

Discussion Questions

1. According to Max Lerner, what are the key elements that make up the American life force? How are these elements reflected in the recreational conduct of the American people?
2. How does the logic of Adam Smith's "invisible hand" reinforce independence of thought and action?
3. In a nation committed to equality of conditions, what is the symbolic significance of public recreation areas?
4. What accounts for the acquisitive nature of recreational conduct in America? Why does it create problems for the stewards and custodians of public recreation?
5. What is meant by the tragedy of the commons? Do you think Hardin's logic is applicable to public recreation settings? Compare Hardin's thinking to that of Adam Smith. In your opinion, what are the strengths and weaknesses of each point of view?

2

The Response

*"And what is happiness?...happiness is
bound up with the satisfaction of desire."*

—**Mark Sagoff**

Seventy miles east of the General Sherman Tree is the tallest
mountain in the United States outside of Alaska. Reaching a summit
of 14,495 feet above sea level, Mt. Whitney stands as a sentinel on
the eastern flank of California's Sequoia National Park. For increasing numbers of Americans, it is both a sight to see and a site to stand
on. There are two main approaches to the top of Mt. Whitney. The
most popular route originates from Whitney Portal on the eastern
slope of the Sierra Nevada. It demands a vigorous uphill hike, but it
can be negotiated in a day or two with time left over for celebrating
the assault in nearby Lone Pine before heading home. A less popular
route originates from the Giant Forest on the western slope of the
Sierra Nevada. It demands an arduous 60-mile trek along the High
Sierra Trail and the John Muir Trail as a prelude to the climb itself.
This approach requires five or six days, and for the stout of heart
there is always the possibility of returning the same way. Having
completed this loop, however, any celebration of Mt. Whitney's as-
cent is understandably muted.

On an early August morning, a Hardin-like figure sits alone on
Whitney's summit. Having made the trek from the Giant Forest, and
having ascended the heights in the middle of the night by moonlight,
the weary hiker basks in the first rays of the eastern sun. It is cold

and crisp to be sure. But there is a bond of warmth between the individual and the mountain. He shouts out Robert Service's poetry for all to hear. Though alone, he is aware of company. He kindly agrees to an encore.

An hour later, the first hikers from Whitney Portal arrive at the summit. It is time to go. There are no words exchanged in the descent, although there is a nagging question in the eyes of many of those still climbing. How much farther to the top? At Trail Crest, where the eastern and western approaches to Mt. Whitney converge for the last two miles to the summit, 136 hikers already have been passed. And looking eastward, a steady stream of ant-like creatures is slowly working its way upward. The reciter of poetry turns to the west.

Maximizing Recreationists' Satisfactions

Hardin's critics are quick to point out a fallacy in the application of the tragedy of the commons argument to recreation areas and facilities. If unlimited access to limited resources inevitably leads to a diminishment in the quality of recreation opportunities and environments, why do people continue to flock to heavily used recreation areas? The answer, they conclude, is obvious. "The crowds enjoy what they find—otherwise they would not come." [1]

Hardin, it seems, is simply trying to foist his values on the American public. When he argues that "we must soon cease to treat the parks as commons or they will be of no value to anyone," [2] what he is really saying is that we must preserve the values he cares for, "but not necessarily the values which most Americans share." [3] Like the solitary hiker on Mt. Whitney, Hardin may aspire to a different experience, but who's to say it's a better one?

In a democracy, they continue, "people want what they want—not what [somebody else] thinks they ought to want. And they should have what they are willing to pay for: Winnebagos, power boats, bowling alleys, movies." [4] Furthermore, park, recreation, and tourism professionals are obliged to maximize satisfactions by accommodating the public's desires. It's our duty. After all, "what argument can be given for failing to satisfy the wants of the ... mass ... ?" [5]

Hardin's adversaries contend further that mutually agreed upon coercion as the only permanent solution to the purported tragedy of the commons is ethically repugnant. [6] We live in a democracy where the process of change is as important as change itself. Moreover, human beings certainly are not as selfish as Hardin would have us believe. People are capable of responding to educational, informational, and interpretive programs. The problem, they avow, is really one of making these programs more effective. Their optimistic motto reads thus: "through interpretation, understanding; through understanding, appreciation; through appreciation, protection." [7]

When all is said and done, Hardin's critics conclude, to the extent that the tragedy of the commons is at all relevant to recreation settings, a conscientious citizenry can be expected to recognize the problem, consider the options open to them, and react in a responsible and democratic manner. Or can they?

Promises and Pitfalls of Human Adaptability [8]

Adaptation is found throughout the natural world and is termed by René Dubos as the "one attribute that distinguishes most clearly the world of life from the world of inanimate matter." [9] It is the ability of an organism to change the environment to make it more fitting, and to change itself through mutation and natural selection toward the same end.[10]

In a general evolutionary context, adaptation is a desirable trait of human development. It allows people to tame vast tracts of uninhabited land, to populate inhospitable climatic regions, and to become immune to certain diseases. Furthermore, when coupled with technological innovation, the adaptable nature of human beings promotes such adjustments at a rapidly accelerating pace. In a world characterized by change, human adaptability ensures a flexibility that is vital to survival.

There is another side to the issue of human adaptability, however, that also deserves attention. It is described by Dubos in his book *Man Adapting*:

The aspect of the problem of adaptation that is probably the most disturbing is paradoxically the very fact that human beings are so adaptable. This very adaptability enables them to become adjusted to conditions and habits which will eventually destroy the values most characteristic of human life. [11]

Dubos illustrates the nature of this problem by discussing the facility with which people have adjusted to the negative properties of urban environments such as air pollution, traffic congestion, and urban sprawl. He cautions that people not only adapt to such elements over time—they eventually define them as normal and then rely on them as bases for further expectations. The direction toward which such a process can lead is depicted by Dubos in a sobering indictment of the urban condition:

Life in the modern city has become a symbol of the fact that [humans] can become adapted to starless skies, treeless avenues, shapeless buildings, tasteless bread, joyless celebrations, spiritless pleasures—to a life without reverence for the past, love for the present, or hope for the future. [12]

The point of Dubos' argument is that a biological view of adaptability is insufficient for human life. There is more to the human condition than just a concern for survival. The way in which humankind survives is an equally important issue. "The uniqueness of [humankind] comes from the fact that [we] do not live only in the present; [we] still carry the past in [our] bodies and in [our] minds, and [we are] concerned with the future." [13] Should we lose sight of that, then the "lowest common denominators of existence tend to become the accepted criteria, merely for the sake of a gray and anonymous peace or tranquility." [14]

Human Adaptability and Recreationist Satisfaction

Dubos' admonition has particular meaning for park, recreation, and tourism professionals who are driven by a commitment to the provision of satisfying recreation opportunities. Is it not possible, after all, that recreationists are adjusting to the negative properties of heavily taxed recreation resources such as crowding, conflict, and environmental degradation without experiencing losses of satisfaction? Is it not also possible that recreationists are growing to expect such conditions, are defining them as normal, and are relying on them as bases for further expectations? Finally, to the extent that recreation planning and management are based on past reports of recreationist satisfaction, is it not even possible that planners and managers themselves are leading the way to that "gray and anonymous peace or tranquility" which so troubles Dubos?

Research concerning the impact of crowding on recreationist satisfaction confirms these suspicions. A number of river recreation studies have revealed that increasingly crowded conditions are having little or no negative effect on participant satisfaction levels. [15, 16, 17] Moreover, similar studies in other settings indicate this finding is not limited to river recreation environments. [18, 19] Furthermore, not only do people appear to be growing less sensitive to crowding in recreation settings, they appear to be growing less sensitive to the environmental deterioration that inevitably accompanies crowding. In a study of boaters and campers visiting the Apostle Islands National Lakeshore in northern Wisconsin, for example, investigators have found that as use levels increase, recent visitors become more tolerant of environmental degradation. [20]

Researchers have explained these findings in the following ways. First, recreationists sensitive to crowding and environmental despoliation may have already moved on to other areas and therefore may not be accounted for in single time frame user studies. Second, repeat visitors are readjusting their expectations to conform to the changing nature of recreation opportunities. And third, new generations of recreationists are expecting greater numbers of people and problems and consequently are more tolerant of them.[21] While the first explanation suggests that some recreationists may not be adapting to increasingly higher user densities and environmental degradation, the second and third accountings indicate they are being displaced by other recreationists who are.

Underpinning this pattern of recreationist "invasion and succession" [22] is a planning and management process that is based largely on what a majority of the people have been satisfied with in the past. Such a process, which tends to define demand in terms of past consumption, [23] precipitates a further decline in the quality of recreation opportunities and environments by promoting more of the same. Roger Clark and his colleagues illustrate how recreation planners and managers contribute to this downward spiral in a discussion of the predicament of displaced campers. "Unfortunately, as the displaced traditionalists move on to increase use at more primitive locations, management may again respond by developing sophisticated facilities, thus attracting less environment-oriented campers and setting in motion another wave of invasion and succession." [24] Thus, out of a concern for providing satisfying recreation opportunities to a majority of users, planners and managers inadvertently support the adaptive process and foster greater environmental damage.

In sum, human adaptability in its recreational context supplies an ironic twist to the tragic scenario portrayed by Hardin. It suggests that however diminished the quality of recreation opportunities and environments may become, a majority of recreationists will be oblivious to it. They will still be satisfied. Given time, their adaptable nature guarantees it. Exacerbating the situation is a planning and management approach that is guided by past reports of recreationist satisfaction. This reactive approach tends to offer only positive reinforcement to the adaptive process. Where it will end is not known, but the words of Edward Abbey foreshadow a likely direction when he speaks of a beautiful mountain scene that needs only a few discarded beer cans to make it look natural. [25]

The Quality Issue

Skeptics may assert that change is inevitable and that the adaptable nature of human beings allows us to accommodate change without sacrificing happiness. They may assert further that quality is a subjective and individual matter and that people who are dissatisfied with existing recreation opportunities and environments need only move on to less crowded and more pristine settings. Both assertions merit consideration.

The first criticism is usually followed by the pronouncement, "You don't miss what you don't know." Practically, this can be made to work only if one disregards any reference to the responsibility of one generation to leave a legacy to succeeding ones. But future generations will probably defile the current one for filling up Glen Canyon with backwater much the same as this generation defiles previous ones for slaughtering bison and stripping the great northern pine forests.

The second criticism is defensible only to the extent that displaced recreationists have an adequate supply of other places to go and that those places are protected by responsible planning and management. But that is not the case. Not only are recreation resources limited in size and kind, recreation planners and managers have been shown to perpetuate their despoliation by providing new opportunities based on what a majority of recreationists have been satisfied with in the past. The direction toward which such a reactive and anthropocentric planning and management process is leading has already been graphically portrayed by Dubos. It is a direction in which "the lowest common denominators of existence tend to become the accepted criteria, merely for the sake of a gray and anonymous peace or tranquility."

What Does Not Weigh in the Balance

The adaptable nature of human beings complicates the issue of the tragedy of the commons. Those who know only the enjoyment of a recreational outing on Lake Powell have little empathy for others who lament the loss of Glen Canyon. To them, life is richer because of the construction of Glen Canyon Dam. So what's the fuss?

More and more the fuss concerns something that traditionally has been left out of land use debates—a concern for the natural environment itself. Historically, such debates have centered only on balancing the competing rights of people to make use of their properties. As Christopher Stone points out in his provocative work *Should Trees Have Standing?* [26] what has not been weighed in the balance are the "rights" of the property per se.

That the environment should possess rights of its own is a concept largely foreign to Western thought. [27] The prevailing Judeo-Christian tradition holds that we are the masters of nature and that it is "God's will to exploit nature for his proper ends." [28] So it is that in America, in heated discussions over the relative quality of a mountain adventure on one's own or in the presence of a hundred others, or in arguments over the degree to which Garrett Hardin's proposed solution to the tragedy of commons compromises democratic rights and principles, it is difficult to imagine someone pausing to reflect on what is not being weighed in the balance. And yet, recalling that solitary figure on the summit of Mt. Whitney, it is disquieting to think that no one is speaking for the company he kept.

Discussion Questions

1. Do you believe park, recreation, and tourism professionals are obliged to serve popular tastes for recreation? Are there exceptions to your answer? If so, under what circumstances?
2. What are the advantages and disadvantages of human adaptability in its recreational context?
3. How might planning for the future based on past consumption contribute to a deterioration in the quality of recreation opportunities and the environment?
4. In your estimation, is there a distinction between a human being and a humane being? What is the nature of the distinction? Why does it matter?
5. What is the essence of quality in recreation opportunities? How can that quality best be maintained by park, recreation, and tourism professionals? What particular problems do you envision in that regard for the stewards and custodians of recreation resources?

3

The Dilemma

"Recreational development is a job not of building roads into lovely country, but of building receptivity into the still unlovely human mind."

—Aldo Leopold

There is a dilemma facing today's park, recreation, and tourism professionals. On the one hand, we feel obliged to serve popular tastes for recreation. On the other hand, by so doing we are contributing to the deterioration of recreation opportunities and environments themselves.

This dilemma is intensified by the democratic climate in which we operate. In a country that champions individual rights, any attempt to limit the public's access to recreation resources or to alter its recreational conduct is bound to cause a ruckus. Such meddling is simply un-American. At the same time, to those who care about environmental quality, it is clear that something must be done. For a profession that takes great pride in being responsive to the needs of people, however, just what that something might be is a source of considerable frustration.

Nevertheless, the task before the park, recreation, and tourism profession is one of reconciling the recreational needs of people with a concern for the environment in which those needs are expressed. It is no mean task because it necessitates tampering with elements of the American life force. Yet it is one that must be undertaken both for the good of the environment and ultimately for the good of the citizenry itself.

Exorcising the Spirit of Adam Smith

As you might expect, Hardin has something to say about this matter. In regard to individual rights, he proposes that "it is clear that independence of individual action will have to be significantly circumscribed. For a century or two, the European variant of Homo sapiens has assumed that the individual is the best judge of [her or] his own welfare, and that the aggregate of individual actions produces the optimal collective welfare. This belief furnishes the supposedly objective justification for asserting individual rights in the use of such non-individually owned resources—'common pool' resources, or commons—as air and water. One has only to listen to the impassioned defense of such 'rights' in a town meeting situation to recognize the religious overtones of the word 'right.' Like the word 'sanctity,' the word 'right' is introduced into the discussion to put an end to the infinite regress of rational inquiry." [1]

To those who continue to cling to Adam Smith's ideals, Hardin adds that "the morality of an act is a function of the state of the system at the time it is performed." [2] In frontier America, the logic of the "invisible hand" was defensible because unlimited resources were being subjected to limited demands. Today limited resources are being subjected to unlimited demands. Under these circumstances, Hardin contends, Adam Smith's thinking backfires.

Sacrificing individual rights for the good of the group, as Hardin would have us do, is nonetheless distasteful to a nation of individuals that emerged in direct rebellion to a European heritage of group tyranny. Yet as Philip Slater argues, "the individual is sacrificed either way. If he [or she] is never sacrificed to the group, the group will collapse and the individual with it [ála the tragedy of the commons]. Part of the individual is, after all, committed to the group. Part of him [or her] wants what 'the group' wants, part does not. No matter what is done some aspect of the individual—id, ego, or whatever—will be sacrificed." [3]

It is not, then, a case of the individual versus the group. Each must make concessions for the welfare of the other. In America the emphasis has been on the group making concessions to the individual. And while such personal liberties should not be treated lightly, it is important to recognize that an accent on individualism is an exception rather than the rule among the world's communities. Quoting Slater again, "we are so accustomed to living in a society that stresses individualism that we need to be reminded that 'collectivism' in a broad sense has always been the more usual lot of [humankind], as well as of most other species. Most people in most societies have been born into and died in stable communities in which the subordination of the individual to the welfare of the group was taken for granted, while the aggrandizement of the individual at the expense of his fellows was simply a crime." [4] So it is that Hardin's prescription for resolving the tragedy of the commons is not really as distasteful as one might imagine. It is prescribed around the world.

Moreover, it is important to understand that it is not individualism per se that is under attack. Rather, it is one form of individualism that must be subordinated to the welfare of the commons. As Nathan Glazer states, "it is clear that some part of American individualism, whether we consider it 'rampant' or 'rugged,' is under severe restraint, and there is no hope that the restraints will become anything but more severe as time goes on. But it is necessary to point out that some kinds of individualism are under restraint only because another aspect of individualism is doing quite well. This is the political aspect of individualism, in which the single individual or individuals organized in private groupings battle for what they conceive to be their rights or a better condition." [5] "Two faces of individualism," Glazer continues, "the more rugged economic and institutional individualism of the United States, hampered and hobbled by a new kind of individualism devoted to self-realization, to the protection of the environment." [6]

Elevating Popular Tastes

Limiting an individual's right of access to recreation areas and facilities is one thing, but attempting to alter her or his recreational conduct is another. Park, recreation, and tourism professionals are understandably sensitive about imposing our values on others. However noble the rationale, how can we do anything but provide the public what it wants?

The problem, of course, is that we have seen where this thinking is leading. By serving popular tastes, park, recreation, and tourism professionals are contributing to the deterioration of recreation opportunities and environments. And for that we must bear some responsibility. As the futurist, Arthur Harkins, admonishes, "inaction is a form of action, a sin of omission so to speak." [7] By serving popular tastes and by assuming a reactive posture, we are helping shape the quality of life. In that sense, we cannot help but impose our values on others.

At the same time, by elevating popular tastes, by promoting recreational conduct that is in concert with environmental quality, park, recreation, and tourism professionals can assume a proactive posture—a sin of commission, perhaps, but at least one that is justifiable in the broader context of environmental integrity.

Taking on such an educational role, as many writers have pointed out, does not undermine a commitment to a democratic political philosophy.[8] We must understand that "aspiration and conventional behavior are in a continual battle. We are willing to impose coercion on ourselves to some degree (as in paying for lessons that we know we may never pursue) precisely because we recognize that left wholly to the pursuit of our routine preferences we are not likely to do and be all that we want. A mixture of autonomy and self-imposed discipline is something we know very well." [9]

Elitism? Bear in mind that whether park, recreation, and tourism professionals are committed to serving popular tastes or elevating them, by our inaction or action, we are helping create the future. Either way we carry with us a measure of responsibility.

The Comedy of Community

There remains the perplexing issue of how best to affect the desired reconciliation between people and the environment. Is "mutual coercion, mutually agreed upon" the only solution to the tragedy of the commons? Is direct regulation of visitor access and visitor behavior the only way to elicit recreational conduct that is in harmony with environmental quality? Is there no room for educational, informational, or interpretive services?

In the short run, contrary to conventional wisdom, [10] coercion may be preferable in deference to the environment. [11] While park, recreation, and tourism professionals traditionally have favored indirect over direct methods of regulating recreational conduct, we have based our position on the assumption that educational processes affect recreationists' attitudes, and that attitudinal changes, in turn, affect behavior. As John Hendee has cautioned, however, the causal relationship between attitudes and behavior is suspect. [12] And to those who are committed to weighing environmental concerns in the balance, "good intentions are no substitute for good performance."[13]

At the same time, there is some evidence to suggest the opposite may be true. That is, it is possible that behavioral change precipitates attitudinal change. Rooted in cognitive dissonance theory and self-perception theory, [14] this school of thought suggests that attitudes evolve to justify behavior in a post hoc manner. Many Americans, for example, came to accept the 55-mile-per-hour speed limit only after having it imposed on them. By complying with the law for several years, they internalized the rationale for its institutionalization. This psychological sequence suggests that coercing people into environmentally sensitive recreational behavior may eventually lead to the establishment of environmentally sensitive recreational attitudes as well. In the meantime, contrary to present trends, the environment would not suffer.

In the long run, however, education promises to play the prominent role in affecting the fundamental change in human values called for by Hardin. And the essence of that education undoubtedly will be wrapped up in what Kenneth Boulding calls the "comedy of community." [15]

"Community is a phenomenon within human society ... by which the identity of the individual becomes bound up with identification with the group or community." [16] This is not a new phenomenon. Tocqueville referred to it as the "principle of self-interest rightly understood" [17] and suggested that humans serve themselves in serving their fellow creatures and that their private interest is to do good." [18] More recently, Aldo Leopold expanded the concept to include the environment when he argued that "when we see land as a community to which we belong, we may begin to use it with love and respect." [19] The power of the idea, then, is in the realization that people are an interdependent part of a larger community of life, and that doing damage to any element of that community is ultimately doing damage to oneself.

"Identity," says Boulding, "is a very powerful source of decisional behavior." [20] "Once people are coerced, or even better, persuaded, into making sacrifices, their identity becomes bound up with the community organization for which the sacrifices were made." [21] The challenge for park, recreation, and tourism professionals is to persuade the American public to make the necessary sacrifices for the sake of the larger ecological community. While such persuasion will take time, it can be undertaken with the confidence that the public's identity eventually will become intertwined with a new sense of community and that they will call it their own.

What are needed, to summarize Boulding's thinking, are some sacred sanctions that overcome the more self-centered images of individual interest. Such sanctions might then prevent the tragedy of the commons because of the community identity which the perception of sacredness creates in the individual. Where there are conflicts between the individual and the community, the sanctions must reconcile them. Where there are compatibilities, they must rejoice in them. Above all else, the sacred sanctions must provide a solid ethical foundation for the future.

Adam Smith's America is, in many respects, bankrupt. Changes must be made in the American life force. Unrestrained individualism must yield to a more temperate code of conduct based on the development of a public ecological conscience. While such changes may be criticized simply as limitations on individual freedom and rights, they deserve a more honest appraisal. For in the final analysis, "we no longer face a physical frontier, but a change in philosophy, a complete reversal of our attitude toward the Earth that might open the door to a golden era far more resplendent than the old." [22]

Discussion Questions

1. Why are park, recreation, and tourism professionals reluctant to limit access to recreation resources? What would Garrett Hardin say to us?

2. Are park, recreation, and tourism professionals obliged to elevate popular tastes for recreation as well as serve them? Explain your thinking.

3. Do you believe that attitudes cause behavior? What are the implications of your answer for the probable effectiveness of informational, educational, and interpretive services in eliciting responsible recreation behavior?

4. Under what circumstances do you believe the direct regulation of recreation behavior (coercion) is justified? How does your answer to this question relate to your answer to the previous question?

5. What is meant by the comedy of community? How might its realization prevent the tragedy of the commons?

Part II

___

EMERGENCE OF A WORTH ETHIC

The concepts of value are profound and difficult exactly because they do two things at once: they join [people] into societies, and yet they preserve for them a freedom which makes them single [individuals]. A philosophy which does not acknowledge both needs cannot evolve values, and indeed cannot allow them.

—Jacob Bronowski

4

A Worth Ethic
for Parks, Recreation, and Tourism

*"Today each of us has a choice. [We] can remain
a statistic, one of the [five]-plus billion, or [we] can
take responsibility for [our] world and attempt to
influence its direction."*

—Raymond Dasmann

Can park, recreation, and tourism professionals contribute to the formulation of the sacred sanctions called for by Kenneth Boulding? Can we contribute to the creation of a new sense of community in the citizens we serve?

Yes, park, recreation, and tourism professionals can contribute. We can develop a philosophy of service based on sacred sanctions of our own making. We can practice and preach that philosophy in a way that will motivate the American people to embrace it as their own. Park, recreation, and tourism professionals can make a difference. But we must step out from the shadow of the masses to lead. And that requires the kind of courage that comes with conviction of purpose.

Part II of this book is intended to fortify park, recreation, and tourism professionals for that leadership role. It develops the concept of a worth ethic as an ideological foundation for service delivery and explores in depth three sacred sanctions, or tenets, upon which the worth ethic is based. Part II, then, is primarily a statement of philosophy. But it is more than that. It is a statement of conviction as well.

Why a Worth Ethic? [1]

There is a saying that one must "earn the respect" of people. Such respect is typically achieved through hard work and perseverance. It is accepted as a given that by such efforts one illustrates one's qualities. And it is accepted further as a consequence that by such qualities one should be measured as a human being. This approach to life, no matter how productive, begs a very important question. Why would one not have the respect of people to begin with?

An emphasis on proving one's self, particularly through work, is deeply embedded in the American way of life. The monumental effort involved in carving a civilization out of the wilderness required that a premium be placed on productivity—productivity through hard work. It is a cultural characteristic that lingers to this day with the result that a person's employment is commonly viewed as his or her primary source of dignity and self-esteem.

A value system based predominantly on work roles, however, is problematic for at least two reasons. First, much employment today requires only a partial commitment of an individual's talents. Tedious, repetitive, piecemeal labor, for example, frequently involves only part of a worker's capabilities. Consequently, any assessment of individual worth based solely on work performance does an injustice to the whole person. Second, the prospect of a post-industrial society in which work as we know it might be the domain of relatively few individuals suggests that a value system based on a work ethic would preclude large numbers of people from experiencing a sense of self-worth. As Don Fabun notes, "the tragedy is not, as some seem to believe, that this way of life may come about well within our lifetimes; the tragedy is that, knowing this, we are doing little or nothing to prepare ourselves or the younger generation to cope with it." [2]

Clearly, the time has come for a new ethic to replace the sanctity of work. While recognizing the importance of an occupation in life, people must not subjugate themselves to it. They must embrace a broader view, one that encourages the fullest expression of all that it means to be human, one that is based on respect to begin with.

Tenets of a Worth Ethic

The replacement of an antiquated work ethic with a worth ethic would require fundamental changes in the way people relate to each other and to the environment in which they live. Such changes may be discussed in light of three tenets basic to the idea of a worth ethic: respect as a birthright, freedom to grow, and opportunities for choice.

Respect as a Birthright
Perhaps the greatest distinction between the work ethic and the proposed worth ethic rests with the belief that the respect customarily afforded people through hard work and perseverance in contemporary life would be earned by them through birth. Resisting the tendency to view people as factors of production in the traditional land-labor-capital scheme, advocates of a worth ethic would revere the intrinsic dignity and worth of being human. And rather than measuring the value of people by their degree of productivity or utility, people would be measured, if at all, by their tenderness, by their compassion, and by their degree of humaneness. In such a social climate, people would not feel compelled to earn the respect of others. On the contrary, they could only earn their disrespect.

Respect for human life is only part of the proposition, however. Proponents of a worth ethic would also extend such respect to all living things. They would recognize that although other life forms have an economic value, they are above all else meta-economic. [3] They have not been created by humans, and it would be presumptuous to assume they have been created expressly for humans. They must, therefore, be viewed primarily as ends in themselves, and they must be viewed with a good deal of respect and with a feeling for their intrinsic value.

This does not suggest that humans do not have dominion over other living beings, nor does it suggest that other life forms should not be appreciated for their economic value. It does suggest, however, that prevailing attitudes toward other members of the ecological community must be changed to reflect a deeper understanding of the interdependence characterizing humankind's relationship with them. It suggests that the word "dominion" carries with it certain obligations as well as countless opportunities. It suggests, as E. F. Schumacher so aptly put it, that "it is no use talking about the dignity of [humankind] without accepting that noblesse oblige." [4]

Freedom to Grow

A logical outgrowth of respect as a birthright is the belief that human beings have an innate right to develop to their fullest potential. While such development cannot be guaranteed, its right to take place can. Recognizing the limitations of work as an avenue for such growth, park, recreation, and tourism professionals can insist on the provision of additional opportunities outside of the work setting. We can insist that people have opportunities to grow and develop through participation in a variety of leisure activities.

Given respect as a birthright, growth through leisure experiences might assume a qualitatively different form than that of today. Since the status that has to be sought in contemporary life would be ascribed to an individual by birth, there would be little need to use leisure as a medium for conspicuous consumption or as a means for proving one's self at the expense of others. Leisure in such times would be free to approach its classical conception as ". . . an act of aesthetic, psychological, religious and philosophic contemplation: a category of activity almost entirely missing from American life today." [5] Growth, consequently, would also be free to take on new meaning. It would not refer to physical expansion through the consumption of economic goods and services, nor would it refer to the accumulation of material wealth. Growth would refer instead to mental or spiritual expansion through the consumption of thoughts and ideas. Growth would refer to the accumulation of knowledge. Its direction would not be outward but inward. And, just as today only with a fundamental twist in its meaning, growth would be valued above all else.

Opportunities for Choice

Respect as a birthright and freedom to grow as basic tenets of a worth ethic are only meaningful if they can be exercised. Clearly, there must be a third tenet, one that is committed to the provision of a diversity of opportunities for human growth and development.

If there is a keyword in parks, recreation, and tourism it would have to be the word "choice." Recognizing the richness of individual differences, park, recreation, and tourism professionals have an obligation to do all that is in our power to ensure continued opportunities for choice—choice among areas, among facilities, and among programs.

The importance of this obligation cannot be overstated. In many respects, leisure is one of the last domains in life where individuals have a great deal of latitude. It is widely recognized that the voluntary nature of the leisure experience is integral to its quality. In a very real sense, then, the element of choice is a precious commodity, one that is central to the value of leisure experiences.

In the final analysis, professionals in our field are managers of opportunities for choice. Although this statement may sound quixotic in an era of seemingly limited resources, it serves to underscore what will undoubtedly become the critical feature of the park, recreation, and tourism profession in years to come.

Max Lerner, the noted columnist and observer of the American scene, was asked some years ago to sum up American civilization in one word. The word he chose was "access." Not freedom, or justice, or equality, but access. He went on to explain that people in the United States were born with unequal abilities, but with equal access to opportunities. And he indicated further that the essence of the American dream involved the continual expansion of such equal access. Lerner's observation was prophetic for our profession, because we have become the stewards of access and the custodians of choice.

Communicating the importance of this role in enhancing the quality of life is paramount to the continued evolution of our profession. It is a message, if Lerner's observation is correct, that can be delivered in defense of the essence of the American experience.

Waving the Flag

Note that the three basic tenets of the proposed worth ethic introduced above—respect as a birthright, freedom to grow, and opportunities for choice—bear some resemblance to the three basic political tenets of America: the right to life, liberty, and the pursuit of happiness. These tenets are held dearly by most Americans.

The implications of this association for parks, recreation, and tourism are encouraging. For it may be that by communicating this resemblance to the American people in a vigorous and united front, sufficient political support can be won to protect the future of this vital area of human service. As with all meaningful campaigns, however, a flag is needed to rally around, a banner is required to illustrate the cause. In the following three chapters, we continue to develop and refine the concept of a worth ethic so it may be meritorious of such service.

Discussion Questions

1. Why is the work ethic increasingly problematic as a basis for valuing human beings?

2. What are the three sacred sanctions that comprise the worth ethic? In your estimation, are they appropriate as cornerstones of service for the park, recreation, and tourism profession?

3. Do you agree with Max Lerner's choice of "access" as the key word to describe the essence of American civilization? If not, what word would you choose? How would your word highlight the mission of the park, recreation, and tourism profession?

4. Do you see a similarity between the worth ethic's basic tenets and America's democratic ideals? How might such a similarity help the cause of our field?

5. Is there an existing banner or flag around which park, recreation, and tourism professionals can rally in support of our cause? If so, what is it, and is it working? If not, is one really necessary?

5

Respect as a Birthright

*"Through respect for life we enter into
a spiritual relationship with the world."*

—Albert Schweitzer

Embracing respect as a birthright as a sacred sanction for parks, recreation, and tourism is an act that should not be engaged in lightly. It brings with it serious ramifications regarding the positions our profession should take on various issues related to the interaction of people with each other and with the environment which supports them. This chapter addresses those ramifications in the contexts of self-respect, respect for others, and respect for all living things.

A Persistent Malady

In 1951, Lewis Mumford published *The Conduct of Life* in which he diagnosed the principal ailment of modern times as a moral breakdown. [1] Mumford attributed the breakdown to the Western world's engrossment with the fabrication of machines and the exploitation of nature while neglecting the proper education of people. Symptoms of the ailment were everywhere—Mumford recalled the Holocaust and Hiroshima. Humankind, while bewitched by its ability to create new tools, was bewildered by the question of how best to put them to use.

It is disheartening to think that 60 years later, Lewis Mumford's diagnosis is still accurate, but there is little evidence to suggest otherwise. Indeed, the mechanistic world of the 1950s has given way to the technocratic world described by Alvin Toffler in *The Third Wave*. [2] Although Toffler is optimistic about the prospects for such a world, others are less so. Alan Drengson, for example, has suggested that in a technocratic state the "production of things becomes more important than persons and communities." [3] And just as nature is exploited for its utilitarian value, so too are people exploited for theirs. One wonders who is in control of such a world, the toolmakers or the tools? Is it really possible, as Mumford quotes Samuel Butler, that humans "may become just a machine's contrivance for reproducing another machine?" [4]

Upon closer scrutiny, it is evident that it is not really an issue of who is controlling whom. To the extent that human beings are being shaped to fit the technological mold, to the extent they are being valued in terms of their contributions to technological processes, and to the extent they are being dehumanized as a result, it is really an issue of what human beings are doing to themselves. Mumford understood this when he said, "we have reached a point in history where [we have] become [our] own most dangerous enemy." [5]

Lest we become too despondent over the prospects for humanity, it stands to reason that if we are indeed our own worst enemy we also have the capacity to make peace with ourselves. And this, in fact, was the essence of Lewis Mumford's prescription for human health 60 years ago. "Only one road lies open to those who would remain human: the road of renewal. Each one of us must dedicate [ourself], at whatever effort, with whatever willing sacrifice, to such a transformation of [ourself] and all the groups and associations in which [we] participate, as will lead to law and order, to peace and cooperation, to love and brotherhood, throughout the planet." [6]

It is high time we take Lewis Mumford seriously. His diagnosis of humankind's spiritual ailment has proven accurate. His antidote may be equally so. We must place our trust in his prescription and put its potency to the test. And to begin with, that means going to the source of the ailment itself—the loss of respect for human life.

Self-Respect

The treatment necessarily begins with the self. The psychiatrist Harry Stack Sullivan reasoned that self-respect is a prerequisite for the adequate respect of others. [7] Sullivan's logic is unsettling in light of the lingering popularity of the work ethic as a basis for the development of individual self-esteem in this country. Not only does an increasingly specialized work world shortchange the value of the whole person, what might happen in the future "when, as some have predicted, two percent of the American population is employed in producing the necessities of life, and 98 percent is not?" [8] Will the vast majority of Americans be stripped of all feelings of self-respect? And how might that affect their respect for others?

Clearly, the problem with the work ethic rests in its utilitarian emphasis. It fails to acknowledge that there is more to the human condition than simply serving as a means to someone else's ends. The ethic that replaces it must not be so limited. It must give a much broader definition to the value of an individual human being. The worth ethic does this. Its interpretation of the value of the individual is rooted in the wisdom of the philosopher Alfred North Whitehead who argued that "everything has some value for itself, for others, and for the whole." [9] People serve utilitarian functions to be sure, but that explains only part of our significance. We are above all else intrinsically valuable. We live not only for others but also for ourselves. We warrant respect, therefore, by virtue of our existence, and we exist because of the occasion of birth.

We park, recreation, and tourism professionals should lose no time in applying the meaning of respect as a birthright to ourselves. After all, a healthy philosophy of service demands for its foundation a high degree of self-respect on the part of the service providers. So fortified, we should be free from the need to prove ourselves to others or to prove ourselves at the expense of others. On the contrary, to paraphrase Sullivan, we should increasingly be able to seek out life experiences that permit us to uncover and demonstrate to our own satisfaction a remarkable capacity for living with and among others. [10]

At the outset, embracing the idea of respect as a birthright contributes to the establishment of a healthy mind set for those of us who deliver park, recreation, and tourism services. Bolstered by our own self-respect, we are better prepared for an open, honest, and accepting relationship with others. We are ready to champion that aspect of humanity which for so long has been overshadowed by a preoccupation with utilitarianism—the intrinsic worth and dignity of being human. We are, in the final analysis, ready to serve by example.

Respect for Others

The extension of respect for oneself to all human beings is the next stage in the evolution of the worth ethic. Its rationale is anchored in the thinking of Albert Schweitzer. In *The Teaching of Reverence for Life*, Schweitzer describes the nature of this stage in the following manner: "I am life that wills to live, in the midst of life that wills to live. The mysterious fact of my will to live is that I feel a mandate to behave with sympathetic concern toward all the wills to live which exist side by side with my own." [11] Accordingly, "ethics consist . . . in my experiencing the compulsion to show to all wills-to-live the same reverence as I do to my own." [12]

Schweitzer's philosophy, which flows from a fundamental reverence for life, has important implications for the park, recreation, and tourism profession because it makes the nature of ethical conduct explicit. "The essence of Goodness," he says, "is: Preserve life, promote life, help life achieve its highest destiny. The essence of Evil is: Destroy life, harm life, hamper the development of life." [13] As will be discussed later on in this book, Schweitzer's conception of goodness constitutes a solid mission statement for our field. For now, however, we would do well to consider its ramifications for the way in which park, recreation, and tourism professionals should relate to the citizens we serve.

The essence of goodness does not mean what is commonly referred to as "doing good" to others. This is a point of confusion because our profession attracts many people who are bent on doing good to others "less fortunate" than themselves. While such feelings appear innocent enough, they reflect an inappropriate orientation to service. Professionals harboring these feelings are not expressing adequate respect for others to begin with. They do not realize that their "do good" philosophy suggests the public's inability to determine what's good for itself. Consequently, rather than doing good, they do a fundamental disservice to those they serve. And more often than not, their constituency is aware of it. Kenneth Boulding makes the point well. "I don't really believe in 'doing good,' because that's insulting to the people you're doing good to." [14]

What is the essence of goodness of which Albert Schweitzer speaks? Quite simply Schweitzer states that "all the goodness one displays toward a living organism is, at bottom, helping it to preserve and further its existence." [15] Park, recreation, and tourism professionals must recognize that just as we live in part for our own purposes, so do others live for theirs. We are obliged, therefore, to respect that in others which we respect in ourselves. And, as shall be detailed in the next two chapters, we must tailor our professional services accordingly.

Respect for others means acknowledging the same intrinsic value in one's fellow human beings that is acknowledged in oneself. Furthermore, it means designing programs that are conducive to the expression of that value. Having recognized this, park, recreation, and tourism professionals can proceed with the confidence that we have taken "the first step in the evolution of ethics . . . an enlargement of the sense of solidarity with other human beings." [16]

Respect for All Living Things

Self-respect and respect for others is not enough, however. Were it so, then the satisfaction of human wants and needs would take precedence over all other considerations. As Eric Katz reminds us, under such circumstances, the continued existence of the natural world would be reduced to a mere contingency. [17] Fortunately, "we are not mere bundles of preferences, but human beings capable of more than desire; we are not merely self-interested consumers bent on achieving the lowest common denominator of satisfaction." [18]

Advocates of the worth ethic respect the world around them. They apply Whitehead's pronouncement that everything has some value for itself, for others, and for the whole to all of life, not just to themselves. They apply Schweitzer's essence of goodness—preserve life, promote life, help life achieve its highest destiny—to all living things, not just to human beings. They understand that they are thereby affirming their interconnectedness and interdependency with all of nature. To echo Christopher Stone, they are giving up some psychic investment in a sense of separateness and specialness in the universe. But in so doing, they are freeing themselves to reach for a higher awareness of what it means to be human. 19

Stepping Off the Pedestal

Respect as a birthright, as we conceive it, does not imply that human beings must "stop at everything" [20] in our interactions with the world around us. Obviously the land and the creatures on it play an instrumental role in the continued livelihood of our species. The question, then, of whether one really respects an animal that is killed for human consumption is left for the philosophers. But what does concern the worth ethic's proponents are the more practical ramifications emanating from this sanction. For example, acceptance of respect as a birthright should lead to a diminishment in the wanton destruction of life. Increasingly, people should begin to realize, as E. F. Schumacher reasoned, that "since consumption is merely a means to human well-being, the aim should be to obtain the maximum of well-being with the minimum of consumption." [21] Emphasis should thus be placed on economizing. Sacrificing life to sustain other life should be carried out with providential care. Harvested resources should be stretched to their limits. These things should happen because of the common understanding that one does not waste what is inherently valuable.

It is certainly possible that the idea of respect as a birthright may contribute to the amelioration of many pressing problems related to a dwindling resource base. But as Stone emphasizes, a new conception of humankind's "relationship to the rest of nature would not only be a step towards solving the material planetary problems; there are strong reasons for such a changed consciousness from the point of making us better humans." [22] Stepping off our self-proclaimed pedestal and assuming a more modest position in the community of life would not be an act of contrition. We would, in the words of Aldo Leopold, simply be changing our role from conquerors of the land-community to plain members and citizens of it. We would be extending respect to our fellow-members and the community as such. 23 And in so doing, we would be expressing a heightened sense of respect for ourselves.

The Possibility of a Universal Community

In the short film *Reflections*, the Earth is pictured from afar through the eyes of Apollo 9's Lunar Module pilot, Russell Schweickart. It is a remarkable movie. As his spacecraft circles the planet, Schweickart speaks of a profound personal transformation. He begins to see the world as it really is. There are no political, cultural, or social boundaries. There are no ideological schisms. There is only one large living blue-green organism. Gradually he begins to see himself differently too. He is not an astronaut, an American, or even a man for that matter, but simply an extension, an antenna of that larger life force in its outward probing. Schweickart is both humbled and delighted by his experience. He has transcended the limitations of his heritage. He has sensed the possibility of a universal community. He will never be the same.

Few of us will ever have the opportunity to experience directly the perspective afforded Russell Schweickart in his orbit of the Earth. But that does not mean we are incapable of undergoing a similar transformation. The same technological know-how that allowed him to see the world as a single living organism has contributed to thousands of other scientific breakthroughs of a similar nature. Increasingly, people are discovering an undeniable ecologic unity to the world. And they are humbled and delighted by their discovery as well. They thereby transcend the limitations of their heritage and perceive the possibility, indeed the inevitability, of a universal community. Individuals who embrace the full meaning of respect as a birthright are among those people. And like the Apollo 9 astronaut, they, too, will never be the same.

Discussion Questions

1. What is the principal ailment of modern people according to Lewis Mumford? Do you agree or disagree with him? Present evidence to support your position.
2. Discuss the value of the individual through the eyes of Alfred North Whitehead. Does his view make sense to you? How does it help clarify the role of park, recreation, and tourism professionals in promoting individual fulfillment?
3. How can Albert Schweitzer's concept of reverence for life be employed in defining the mission of the park, recreation, and tourism profession?
4. According to Schweitzer, what is the essence of goodness? How can it lead to an understanding of ethical recreation conduct?
5. Why is the idea of a universal community important? What are the prospects for its realization? How can park, recreation, and tourism professionals contribute to its fruition?

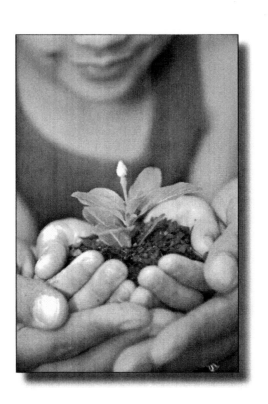

6

Freedom to Grow

"A ship in a harbor is safe, but that is not

what ships are built for."

—Shedd

The relationship between respect as a birthright and freedom to grow is symbiotic. If we truly see and value something for itself, then we recognize its right to develop to its fullest potential. Conversely, if we recognize the right of something to develop to its fullest potential, then we truly see and value it for itself. [1] This symbiotic relationship forms the backbone of the worth ethic. It must be nurtured, however, if it is to support the full weight of a professional philosophy of service. And that is the task of the present chapter.

These pages build on the preceding ones by examining the meaning of freedom and growth in a society tempered by respect as a birthright. Attention is then directed to the implications associated with freedom to grow for the delivery of park, recreation, and tourism services.

What It Means to Be Free

In *The Challenge of Leisure*, Charles Brightbill devotes his final chapter to the issue of freedom. [2] Freedom, while acclaimed widely as an indispensable democratic value, eludes easy definition. Brightbill argues that freedom cannot simply mean the license to do as one pleases, because the actions of one individual commonly interfere with the freedoms of another. Garrett Hardin would agree. But Americans in general are reluctant to concede this point, even when they recognize their own encroachment on the rights of others. Anyone who has inhaled unwillingly the smoke from someone else's cigarette understands this. Freedom must mean something more.

According to Brightbill, freedom has certain benchmarks. "Freedom is something specific. When we speak of freedom, it is freedom to do some particular thing or to be free from something specific. We want to be free to speak our minds about the actions of those who govern us, free to go where we please and to choose our own company. We want to be free from this threat or that control, this burden or that problem—but always it is freedom in relation to something definite and not just everything in general." [3] Freedom cannot mean the liberty to do as one pleases in any situation. It cannot be absolute. Freedom must be qualified.

"Freedom," Brightbill continues, "also means that we have a choice to make and that its determination rests with us. If there is no chance for selection, no alternative, then there is no freedom." [4] This was Aldo Leopold's point when he lamented, "Of what avail are forty freedoms without a blank spot on the map?" [5] There is an inherent tension to the concept of freedom. On the one hand, the more choices there are, the more freedom there is. On the other hand, the more freedom there is, the more chances of collisions. If the collisions are severe enough or frequent enough, society intervenes through its system of laws to restrict the freedom in question. To expand the metaphor, think of the rules that have been set up by society to restrict the free flow of traffic. They do indeed impinge on the freedom of the individual driver. But if you consider the testimony of Kenneth Boulding, they also do more than this. "I accept the limitation of the traffic light. We all stop for a red light. This is a limitation of our freedom, but we accept it because we recognize that it is a limitation which in effect produces more freedom."[6] Boulding's point is forceful. Imagine the free-for-all that would ensue if the traffic signals were removed. Freedom, in its extreme, leads not to the good life, but to anarchy.

At the same time, as Brightbill admonishes, taking away individual freedoms is something that should be done grudgingly. "Almost every minute of our lives is regulated or routinized by something or somebody." [7] Brightbill obviously is troubled by the facility with which society wields its powers of arbitration in matters of personal liberty. But then so is Boulding. "Society's 'shalt nots,'" he says, "are the fences we erect to keep people from the cliff's edges. Falling over cliffs is the worst possible method of learning about them. The trouble is that in the past we have built fences where there are no cliffs." [8] Societal control, taken to its extreme, does not lead to the good life either.

Clearly, some sort of balance is in order. But what is to be its nature? How can freedom be qualified in a way that will help guide people in their specific behaviors? We believe the answer is embedded in a multiplicity of ideas that have been addressed previously in this work; particularly in Tocqueville's principle of self-interest rightly understood, in Boulding's comedy of community, in Mumford's prescription for human renewal, in Whitehead's conception of intrinsic worth, in Schweitzer's reverence for life, and in Leopold's land ethic. Freedom, as we interpret it, is bound up in the awareness that human beings are both wholes and parts. Freedom is appreciation of the fact that human fulfillment hinges on the realization of one's potentials both as an individual and as a member of the larger community of life. Freedom is the recognition that people have a right to live for themselves as long as their lifestyles do not jeopardize the larger existence of which they are but a part. Ultimately, freedom is an opportunity to live one's life in compatibility with the lives of others. And just as importantly, it is an obligation to do so. [9]

Too many people define freedom only as an opportunity. They understand that freedom has much to give but they do not understand that it also has much to take. [10] Freedom exacts a price. The price is responsibility for one's actions. Those who fail to pay the price are not really free. They are merely irresponsible.

Society, on the other hand, often acts as if freedom were only an obligation. It understands that freedom demands much but it does not understand that freedom must give much in return. Freedom exacts a price from society as well. The price is functional autonomy for the individual. A society that fails to pay the price is not really free. It is repressive. It makes a habit out of building fences where there are no cliffs.

German philosopher Friedrich Hegel is credited with saying, "Freedom is the recognition of necessity." [11] The great need of the present day is to recognize the interdependency among all forms of life on Earth and to live in the light of that recognition. If, in the words of Charles Brightbill, we can "grow up" [12] to that responsibility, humankind indeed will be more free.

What it Means to Grow

"Freedom we say—but freedom for what? Do we mean freedom to go as far as we wish in accumulating money or achieving prestige? Freedom to eat, drink, or gossip to our heart's content? Freedom to harass our children or impose upon the good nature of our friends? What is freedom for if not mainly to improve the quality of our lives, to afford the chance to live more abundantly? Freedom ought to substitute the full life for the barren and nurture self-expression." [13]

Brightbill is right. Freedom ought to contribute to human fulfillment through the nurturance of self-expression. It ought to serve as an avenue for growth. But in a society governed by respect as a birthright, what does the word "growth" really mean?

Historically, growth has been defined in economic terms. "The development of production and the acquisition of wealth have thus become the highest goals of the modern world. …" [14] Freedom to pursue those goals has resulted in a society that is indeed rich in things. And for that, Adam Smith deserves credit. At the same time, Lewis Mumford's reference in the preceding chapter to the Western world's spiritual impoverishment makes one question the appropriateness of an economic yardstick as a measure of the full life. Not only is economic prosperity becoming increasingly difficult to sustain (there are fewer things to be divided among more people who want them), the philosophy of materialism is itself under attack. More and more, people are beginning to question the wisdom of the goal of economic growth. As Nathan Glazer observes, "the economic individualist has … lost his former arrogance. Very likely his own children are to be found among the passionate defenders of consumer rights, the environment, women, and minorities. And the economic individualist is hard put to justify himself. Having praised without question the virtues of abundance and continuous growth, he is at a loss when the simple question is put: 'why'?" [15]

The shortcomings of a materialistic way of life are becoming increasingly apparent. A new yardstick is in order. [16] Philip Slater speaks to its design in discussing the birth of a new culture. "What is significant in the new culture is not a celebration of economic affluence but a rejection of its foundation. The new culture is concerned with rejecting the artificial scarcities upon which material abundance is based. It argues that instead of throwing away one's body so that one can accumulate material artifacts, one should throw away the artifacts and enjoy one's body." [17] To measure the full life in this culture, one does not employ a yardstick that gauges richness in things. On the contrary, one employs a yardstick that gauges richness in feelings, experiences, and human relationships. And movement up its scale, too, is understood to be an indication of human growth and development.

However, in contrast to the materialistic world, the new culture of which Slater speaks is "based on the assumption that important human needs are easily satisfied and that the resources for doing so are plentiful." [18] The issue of scarcity that pervades our lives can thus be seen as a relative one (see chapter 9 for an expanded discussion). People have reason for optimism based on a dramatically different conception of what abundance, growth, and fulfillment can mean in a world that affords its residents respect as a birthright.

Growth, in particular, is free to take on new meaning. Detached from its association with things, growth means expanded comprehension and knowledge. Growth means the enlargement of one's "psychic income"; [19, 20] that is, one's increasing ability to receive stimuli from the surrounding environment, to understand that environment, and to appreciate it. Growth means consumption and fulfillment of an entirely new order. And most important of all, it occurs in productive harmony with the growth of others. This "great dream, that of finally growing into the vast world of comprehension and knowing, is … very much alive. This is the grandest dream of all." [21]

Why Freedom to Grow is Important

Freedom to grow is critical to the conceptualization of the worth ethic. The importance of a sense of freedom in life has been stressed by numerous writers. [22, 23] People want to be free to exercise control over their lives. [24] They want to experience a sense of efficacy. They want to make a difference. Research has shown that the absence of such feelings may even contribute to the deterioration and eventual demise of human beings. [25] Freedom is a tenet central to existence in the Western world.

Growth is equally so. The full life alluded to by Brightbill is a product of the growing process. And the growing process, according to Alexander Martin, is contingent on the existence of two conditions: inner-directed effort and relaxation. [26] These are the complementary phases of the creative cycle. And it is this creative cycle that has given us the enduring forms of art, technology, music, literature, religion, and philosophy which we now enjoy. [27]

In sum, freedom to grow enables humankind to exercise the creative cycle. It enables humankind to reach out, explore, experiment, and strive for a fuller life. It enables humankind to create culture. If we are to grow, we must have room. Freedom gives us that room. It is an avenue, an opportunity, an open space, and—lest we forget—a blank spot on the map.

What Freedom to Grow Means for Parks, Recreation, and Tourism

Why, in particular, should freedom to grow be adopted as the second sacred sanction for the park, recreation, and tourism profession? What are its implications for the delivery of services? How can it guide professionals in the administration of their duties? These are the questions to which we now turn.

We live in an age of regulation. [28] The Western world is characterized by a preoccupation with time, routinization, and mass production. While the impacts of such a regulated lifestyle on the individual are varied, it is not uncommon to know people who are resigned to putting in their time, putting up with the routinization, and putting out a product or service of indifferent quality. They are motivated largely by the external rewards of prestige and profit. Their work is stressful. They are, as Philip Slater reminds us, sacrificing their lives for the accumulation of dead things. [29]

It is precisely because the regulated world offers limited opportunities for the individual to exercise the freedom to grow that it is needed as a cornerstone of service for the park, recreation, and tourism profession. Recall that the growing process is dependent on inner-directed effort and relaxation. But the regulated world is predominantly other-directed and stress laden. It is in one's leisure that the conditions are ripe for exercising the creative cycle. It is in leisure that one is freest to grow as a human being. Park, recreation, and tourism professionals cannot guarantee human growth. That is a matter of individual responsibility. But we can work to provide the room. And that is our challenge. We must recognize the right of people to recreate for themselves as long as their recreation does not jeopardize the larger existence of which they are but a part. We must then do all that is in our power to expand those opportunities for the citizens we serve. This we are obliged to do in our capacity as the stewards of access.

At the same time, park, recreation, and tourism professionals must assume responsibility for the welfare of the social and natural environment in which recreational pursuits take place. We must encourage recreational conduct that is compatible with that environment. Where there are incompatibilities (collisions) that are severe enough or frequent enough, the profession must intervene through its developing system of indirect and direct controls to restrict or redirect the recreational conduct in question. [30] This can be done with the confidence that it will, in effect, produce more freedom (remember the limitation of the traffic light). [31] And more freedom means more choices. This we are obliged to do in our capacity as custodians of choice.

At the heart of the matter is the problem of determining when incompatibilities are severe enough or frequent enough to warrant intervention. It is a problem that has received much attention in the outdoor recreation literature in the context of recreational carrying capacity. But it by no means is a problem that is limited to outdoor recreation. Any recreational conduct that infringes on the rights of others warrants scrutiny for possible modification or restriction.

Of an even more troublesome nature is the problem of determining if an incompatibility exists. The first two authors, for example, have argued elsewhere for the establishment of "no rescue" wilderness areas where recreationists would be completely on their own. [32, 33, 34, 35, 36] Critics of the proposal have attacked it largely on humanitarian grounds. [37, 38] But what could be more humane than affording individuals who wish to assume complete responsibility for their own behavior, who wish to accept fully the consequences of their own actions, who wish to live totally for themselves, an opportunity to do so? As long as their recreational conduct is not intruding on the rights of others, whose business is it other than their own?

The park, recreation, and tourism profession, as an instrument of society, must give people room to grow. If it is to extend true freedom to them, it must recognize their right to succeed and to fail. And it must afford them opportunities to exercise that right. This must be done out of respect for the individual.

The individual, in turn, has an obligation to make use of that freedom in a constructive way. Life should be lived in compatibility with the lives of others. Freedom provides the opportunity to live up to that obligation. But there are no assurances. There are no guarantees. There are chances to be taken. There are decisions to be made. Freedom is indeed a risky proposition. But who would have it any other way?

Discussion Questions

1. Why must freedom to grow be qualified as a sacred sanction for the park, recreation, and tourism profession? What is the nature of the qualification?
2. Discuss freedom both as an opportunity and as an obligation. In your opinion, do most people understand the dualistic nature of the concept? How can a misunderstanding cause problems?
3. Why is economic growth problematic as an overriding goal for human beings? How can growth be redefined in a way that is compatible with the world in which we live?
4. How does freedom to grow enable humankind to exercise the creative cycle? Why is leisure critical to this process?
5. What is society's obligation to the individual in providing freedom to grow? What is the individual's obligation to society in exercising that freedom?

7

Opportunities for Choice

*"The appetites which nurture the soul, enlighten the mind,
and generally refresh us can only flourish where there is the
opportunity for expression that emanates from free choice
motivated by personal satisfaction."*

—Charles Brightbill

Respect as a birthright and freedom to grow as basic tenets of
the park, recreation, and tourism profession are important only if
they are activated. There must be a third tenet, one that catalyzes the
first two. Opportunities for choice does that.

This chapter underscores the significance of opportunities for
choice. It then calls for the provision of a diversity of park, recreation, and tourism opportunities by the government. Finally, it
defines the role of the park, recreation, and tourism profession in
managing those opportunities.

A Rude Awakening

In the summer of 1967, the first author was an undergraduate
student at the University of Michigan in Ann Arbor. The pace of
summer school, much like the weather, was slow and relaxed. The
subject was French and it, too, fit the mood of the season. The daily
routine consisted of a morning class and an afternoon of studying on
a north-facing apartment balcony (basking, of course, in the sum-

mer sun). French was spoken. Wine was sipped. Every day it was the same thing. *Toujours la même chose.* It was nice. From the perch on the balcony it was possible to gaze upon the Huron River as it meandered through Ann Arbor. And on clear days, the summer's greenery could be seen in the hills to the north and east of the city. On those days, if one wanted to, it was even possible to see all the way to Detroit. Or so it seemed.

In late July of that summer, on a clear day, the French and the wine were disrupted by the sight of smoke far to the northeast. Something was happening. A nearby radio was switched into service. Something indeed was happening. Detroit was on fire.

The urban riots of the 1960s, as the student was to learn several years later, provide strong direct evidence in support of the value of park, recreation, and tourism services to the American public. In the wake of those riots, the Kerner Commission identified the principal factors contributing to the civil upheaval. Included among them was "poor recreation facilities and programs;" [1] not as an appendage, not as an afterthought, but as one of the major contributing factors. Somehow, someone had forgotten that in a nation committed to equality of conditions, public parks and playgrounds serve an equalizing function. Somehow, someone had forgotten that regardless of one's station in life, one has the right of access to these resources. Somehow, someone had forgotten that they are the poor person's property. The residents of Detroit's ghetto had not forgotten. And they set out to destroy their own community in protest.

It was indeed a rude awakening. But just as shocking was the Kerner Commission's failure to acknowledge the importance of park, recreation, and tourism services in its subsequent recommendations for action. Although poor recreation facilities and programs were listed as a major grievance in 17 of 20 cities experiencing disturbances, [2] only lip service was paid to their rectification. As Richard Kraus described it, "the lack of any recommendation in this area indicates that the Commission failed to assign any real priority to it in its own deliberations and conclusions." [3]

Parks, recreation, and tourism as frosting. It's a perspective all too familiar to those who devote their careers to the ideals of this field—a perspective that is confronted on a daily basis. It is a perspective that spurred David Gray and Seymour Greben into writing their challenging "Future Perspectives" [4] in 1974, and then its sequel "Future Perspectives II: The 1980s and Beyond." [5] It is a perspective that still, more than 40 years after Detroit, is in dire need of repair. *Quel dommage.*

Parks, Recreation, and Tourism and the Public Good

Why is it that park, recreation, and tourism services have failed to earn their rightful place in the national priorities? [6] Why is it they have been so easily dismissed by public policymakers in economically difficult times? Why is it they have not been treated with the respect they deserve?

There appear to be several reasons. Certainly the preeminence of work is one of them. Participation in park, recreation, and tourism programs is valued largely for its recuperative effects, ergo its instrumental effects. Recreation restores people for productivity in other areas of their lives. It is viewed by many, then, as a means to an end rather than as an end in itself. And that suggests, however subconsciously, importance of a secondary nature.

But there is more to it than that. The benefits resulting from recreation engagements are hard to measure. The economic yardstick is calibrated for things. It is not well suited for gauging the psychological rewards associated with recreational experiences. And in Western society, that which is hard to measure is equally hard for many people to value.

Compounding the problem is what Marion Clawson and Jack Knetsch term the "social externalities in consumption" [7] issue. In other words, are there measurable benefits accruing to society as a result of an individual's recreational involvement? According to Clawson and Knetsch, those answering "yes" believe that "recreation is essential to a full and well-balanced personal life; that those who participate in ... recreation tend to become better adjusted socially and better and more productive citizens; and thus the welfare of the whole nation is enhanced. According to this argument, everyone benefits in some way, and even those who do not partake of ... recreation have an interest in its ready availability, and should be willing to help pay for it." [8] Clawson and Knetsch concede that there is something to this argument. "The unresolved question," they say, "is, how much?" [9] Again it appears to be a measurement problem. And in the absence of good data—.

Skeptics of the park, recreation, and tourism profession's contributions to the public welfare thus base their suspicions on the scarcity of direct supportive evidence. The Kerner Commission report aside, there are few facts that lead to the deduction that these services should be treated as a genuine public good. Only time and a substantial amount of empirical evidence can quell that skepticism. (Indeed, empirical evidence of the individual and social benefits resulting from park, recreation, and touristic engagements is just now beginning to mount both in the United States and Canada.) [10, 11]

In the meantime, there is a tremendous store of circumstantial evidence that suggests the indispensable nature of park, recreation, and tourism services to the quality of life. This indirect evidence ranges from the vast sums of money spent on recreation by the general public to countless testimonials by individual citizens describing the positive role of recreation in shaping their lives. This evidence can and should be employed as well in arguing the case for public recreation. Recall, for example, that culture creation is fundamentally a product of leisure pursuits. If it is desirable for all citizens to reach out, to explore, to experiment, to strive for a fuller life; if it is desirable for them to exercise the creative cycle; then it seems eminently reasonable for government to provide a basic range of opportunities for them to do so—if only for the social benefits.

This does not mean that government must concern itself with the provision of all park, recreation, and tourism services. It does mean, however, that it has an obligation to furnish a spectrum of areas, facilities, programs, and personnel to ensure that no person is deprived of the opportunity for choice because of an inability to pay or a disability to play. It means that government must recognize its responsibility to give the individual room to grow through a diverse system of leisure opportunities. This government is obliged to do in its capacity as the guarantor of freedom.

We believe in public recreation and a corresponding governmental responsibility for the provision of recreation services. [12] We believe recreation should be treated as a public good, not as a discretionary item. [13] We believe "willingness to play" should be the key to recreation participation, not "willingness to pay." We believe park, recreation, and tourism professionals should be servants of the public, not sellers of wares. We believe these things not because of the direct evidence, which is admittedly sparse, but because of the indirect evidence, which is convincing in its abundance. That evidence, plus the lingering memory of smoke far to the northeast of Ann Arbor, provides the basis for our conviction.

Managing Opportunities for Choice

What should be the role of park, recreation, and tourism professionals in managing opportunities for choice? What should be our orientation to service? What should we be striving for?

The responsibility is three-fold. First, as mentioned in the preceding chapter, park, recreation, and tourism professionals are obliged to expand opportunities for choice. This obligation is rooted in the basic philosophy that more choice is better than less choice.[14] The professional's job is to expand the realm of recreational choices open to people. "Such expansion is theoretically limitless because it is based on the subjective impressions of individuals as to what is good for them in the area of their own voluntary kinds of activities."[15]

Implicit in this view is the idea that the professional's responsibility is greater than that of simply responding to expressed demand for recreation opportunities. It includes the stimulation of demand as well through the active expansion of recreational choices. To meet this responsibility, the professional is obliged to find out what is going on and then to get ahead of it. "This means a lot of research, a lot of forecasting, and a lot of design work."[16] This means breaking new ground. The goal of this aspect of service should be to develop an ever-expanding system of park, recreation, and tourism opportunities within which all citizens can find meaningful and constructive uses of their leisure time.[17]

Second, again as mentioned in the preceding chapter, park, recreation, and tourism professionals are obliged to intervene on those occasions where there are collisions between or among recreationists or where recreational conduct is jeopardizing the larger existence. This responsibility requires a continual refinement of indirect and direct methods of intervention. The goal of this aspect of service should be to reduce collisions in as inoffensive a manner as possible.

Third, and most importantly, park, recreation, and tourism professionals are obliged to educate the public regarding recreational choices that are in harmony or disharmony with their larger existence. [18] Ideally, we should educate people in such a way that their recreation will lead to social and environmental awareness, sensitivity, responsibility, and protection, and that they will like it. [19] Such education, however, should be motivated out of a concern for enhancing the public's capacity to choose rather than as a strategy for limiting choices.

The role of the park, recreation, and tourism professional is to be the guardian, the preserver of choice, knowing full well that many of those choices may not be "good" in any normative sense. As long as the choices are not outlawed by society, park, recreation, and tourism professionals are obliged to accommodate them. The ultimate responsibility for informed recreational choices must rest with the individual.

We believe the park, recreation, and tourism profession's philosophy of service must be grounded in ecological principles, not in merchant values. We believe the rewards of service must be measured by the extent to which responsible recreationists are cultivated, not by the extent to which dollars and cents are generated. We believe the park, recreation, and tourism profession's primary responsibility must include educating the public as well as catering to it. We believe these things in spite of current economic and political indicators to the contrary. Our conviction resides in our faith in the people who serve this profession; people who understand the unique role of parks, recreation, and tourism in enhancing the quality of human life; people who can put that understanding into powerful words and deeds.

Prospects for the Future

It is easy to be pessimistic these days about the prospects for the future. The media routinely brings home news of international conflict, crime, disease, and poverty. Workers are unhappy. Resources are on the wane. The environment is polluted. And there is the ever- present specter of a nuclear catastrophe. It is indeed easy to be pessimistic these days.

But there are good forces at work too. The park, recreation, and tourism profession is one of them. It doesn't get the attention, it doesn't get the press, because it is a profession that focuses on what is right with people. It serves human health. Of course, we human beings are notorious for taking our health for granted. So don't be dismayed by a lack of support for park, recreation, and tourism services. The citizenry has yet to appreciate their preventive power. But they will in time with your tutelage.

Our profession symbolizes a more hopeful prospect for the future; the prospect of a universal community populated by a humanity that has made peace with itself. [20] We have an integral part to play in shaping that future. By practicing and preaching the philosophy of the worth ethic, perhaps we can even lead the way. It is an ethic that is filled with respect and freedom and choice, ideals which are bound up intimately with a democratic way of life. Like all ethics, however, it must stand the test of time.

Part III of this book initiates that testing period. It explores several paths open to park, recreation, and tourism professionals in our advancement into the 21st century; paths leading to an enhanced professional image, to the creation of new resources, to increasingly relevant professional preparation, and ultimately to better serving the human potential. They are paths that are just now beginning to be blazed in the light of the worth ethic.

Discussion Questions

1. Why have park, recreation, and tourism services failed to earn their rightful place in the national priorities? What can be done about it?
2. In your opinion, should recreation be treated as a public good? Why or why not? What are the implications of your answer for the role of government as the guarantor of park, recreation, and tourism services?
3. What is the three-fold responsibility of the park, recreation, and tourism profession in managing opportunities for choice?
4. Do you accept the idea that more choice is always better than less choice? Explain your thinking.
5. In what way does the park, recreation, and tourism profession serve human health?

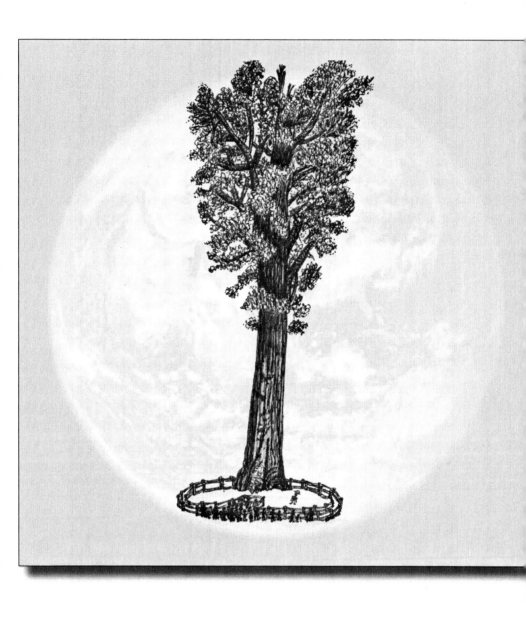

Part III

PATHWAYS TO THE FUTURE

"

[We] master nature not by force but by understanding
. . . we have learned that we gain our ends only with the
laws of nature; we control [nature] only by understanding [its] laws . . . we must be content that power is the
byproduct of understanding. **"**

—**Jacob Bronowski**

8

Breaking the Language Barrier

*"We must acknowledge the power of language to frame
our discussions, lead us to certain conclusions while excluding
others, and limit us without our realization. Our language,
metaphors, models, and theories must begin to reflect the world in
all of its complexities, diversities, richness, and wealth..."*

—Karen Fox

The power of language is awesome. In its most positive sense, language serves as a medium for sharing experiences and expanding the boundaries of knowledge. In this sense, language is a barrier breaker, a vehicle for enlarging our understanding of the world through meaningful communication with others.

Language also can act as a barrier to meaningful human interaction. It can diminish our understanding of the world by obstructing the sharing of experiences and constricting the boundaries of knowledge. This is the power of language in its most negative sense.

Those who desire to lead the park, recreation, and tourism profession must understand the power of language and its potential to be either a positive or negative force in shaping the future. Such understanding requires an examination of the way in which we employ language, a process most of us take for granted. Lest we remain nonchalant about this process, bear in mind that "nothing is more important to a society than the language it uses." [1]

The Park, Recreation, and Tourism Language Barrier

"The first thing to realize is that meanings rest more in people than in words themselves. Words are symbols, which each of us interprets, often in very different ways."[2] Consider, for example, the word "recreation." "To most people, the term 'recreation' evokes highly specific images: of playground asphalt and scuffed paths of softball diamonds, of bicycling and picnics, and trips to the beach. In the main, the public mind associates recreation with organized group activities, physical fitness, and diversion—with 'fun and games,' if you will, which take place in spare time. Recreation is viewed as a beneficial, but peripheral, social activity."[3] On the other hand, "To the thoughtful professional, the role of recreation in leisure is something quite different. It is an ingredient essential to the nourishment of the 'whole person' and an emerging vital means of maintaining a stable and civil society. In this view, the 'fun and games' aspects of recreation do play a role, but a rather minor one."[4]

The first lesson to be learned from a study of language is that the definitional problem with recreation is rooted not so much in the word itself as it is in the discrepancy between the public's interpretation of its meaning and the profession's. Until that discrepancy is eliminated, the word "recreation" is not likely to contribute to barrier breaking. On the contrary, confusion over its meaning is likely to result in it becoming a barrier itself to the advancement of the park, recreation, and tourism profession.

This lesson also has meaning for the self-perceptions of individuals who offer service in the name of recreation because the words we use to describe our role or function in society can shape the way we feel about ourselves.[5] Given the low status afforded the word "recreation" by the general public, it is not surprising that we park. recreation, and tourism professionals are somewhat insecure and defensive about our station in life.

It is tempting to suggest that a solution to these problems would be for our profession simply to communicate our interpretation of recreation to the public in a way that persuades them to alter their interpretation. However, a more detailed examination of the power of existing language reveals this suggestion to be much easier said than done.

"Language is not merely a reproducing instrument for voicing ideas but rather is itself a shaper of ideas."[6] In our continuous effort to organize the "kaleidoscopic flux of impressions" [7] presented to us by our surrounding environment, we categorize and classify those impressions. In other words, we label them or in most instances ascribe them to categories or classifications for which we already have labels. This process is most noticeable, and often most amusing, in the language of children. Several years ago, for example, one of our own children, upon seeing a bird feeder for the first time, exclaimed proudly, "Look, daddy, a bird restaurant!" Our language thus plays an influential role in determining how we will perceive something new to our experience and what we will call it.

There are two byproducts of this labeling process that have important implications for the word "recreation." First, labeling generally results in a simplification or distortion of phenomena. [8] And second, once something is labeled, we tend not to see beyond the label. [9] Therapeutic recreation specialists, in particular, should appreciate the impact of these byproducts since they devote much effort to enabling their clients to overcome the stigmas associated with labeling. An individual labeled "mentally retarded," for example, is often not given credit for possessing other positive human attributes. Moreover, that same individual may not be given a chance to express his or her humanity because of the public's disinclination to look beyond the label. In such instances, labeling "seems to blind us to what we would have seen if we hadn't learned the name." [10]

In sum, while labeling may be explained by the necessity for efficient mental processing in a world characterized by "information overload,"[11] it contributes to a narrowness of thought. Unfortunately, "When our categories become narrowed, our perceptual world may become narrowed, too."[12]

The resulting lesson is sobering for park, recreation, and tourism professionals who hope to change the public's interpretation of recreation. It suggests a tremendous inertia in existing language and consequently tremendous difficulty in changing the meaning of its labels. It suggests that those who would have the public see recreation in a new light must overcome all that it has meant to them in the past, however simplified, however distorted. It suggests that the public may not be cooperative, that they may not really want to look beyond their own definition of recreation, and that they may never be able to see in the word recreation what our profession wants them to see. Such is the power of language in its most negative sense.

The Profession's Dilemma

What should we do? Most thoughtful professionals would argue that we should do something. Rettie implores us to "do away forever with that restrictive tag of 'fun and games' which is our ripe albatross, which impels too many of us to hide meekly behind the coattails of others."[13] Gray and Greben argue even more adamantly that:

> Our traditional definitions of recreation do not advance our understanding of it. For thirty or forty years or more the Park and Recreation Movement has been deluded by a false sense of recreation. This has warped our services, given us false priorities, prevented effective evaluation of results, and inhibited our ability to interpret what we do. Worst of all, it has prevented us from developing an understanding of our goals and methods. The popular understanding of recreation in our field cannot sustain further development. The concept is bankrupt.[14]

Park, recreation, and tourism professionals are clearly in a linguistic predicament. We are bogged down in language that is being translated differently by different people. We are being held back by our own vocabulary, a vocabulary that is subject to a myriad of interpretations. And finally, we are being victimized by a process we decry vehemently when it victimizes others, the process of labeling.

The amount of professional frustration resulting from these linguistic difficulties would be hard to measure. Nonetheless, it would be equally hard to deny that many of the current problems besetting parks, recreation, and tourism are rooted in communication disorders of one sort or another. The fact that we are still debating what "recreation is. ..." [15] within our own ranks, for example, reflects the urgent need for internal linguistic housekeeping before we can expect the public to respond favorably to our pronouncements about the value of our services.

Well, what can we do? Perhaps our study of language will help. We have highlighted its pitfalls. It is now time to turn to its promises.

Breaking the Park, Recreation, and Tourism
Language Barrier

"A person who is mature in [her or] his semantic habits will avoid being perceptually bound to language and will attempt to see the world rather than read it." [16] A futurist named Arthur Harkins is such a person. Referring to the current park and recreation language problem, Harkins notes that "when social designers are confronted with a linguistic barrier, they sometimes have to invent language to allow them to get around that barrier and to proceed." [17] He goes on to say that "there ought to be a term invented by you people to get us around the limitations imposed by the work/leisure conceptual dichotomy. Somehow you need to come up with a word that's good for the ... the 21st [century], one which blends those two concepts. Then, by virtue of that word's metaphorical power at first, and later on its design and planning power, we might accordingly begin to redefine the contributory potentials of people." [18]

Harkins offers us a way out of the predicament imposed by our current linguistic barriers. He tells us quite simply to invent new language to describe our reason for being. In addition, he underscores what we should by now be fully aware of; the metaphorical power of such language has the potential to shape the public's future attitude toward our profession. The concept of a worth ethic has evolved from Harkins's way of thinking. It is new language that has been designed to express the essence of the park, recreation, and tourism profession. Since it is new symbolism, meaning will flow from the profession's initial interpretation of it. Furthermore, the idea of a worth ethic capitalizes on the "'as-if' quality of metaphor"[19] by asking people to behave as if respect is a birthright, as if freedom to grow is guaranteed, and as if opportunities for choice are to be maximized. As the worth ethic and its tenets are repeated over time, the as-if quality should disappear, resulting in public acceptance of the concept as is. If the worth ethic is adopted as a banner for our profession, its acceptance may then be transferred to the profession itself and ultimately to the people who serve it. Such would be the power of language in its most positive sense.

The Future's Language

The potential of language should now be clear. Language is a tool for those who aspire to shape the park, recreation, and tourism profession. Like all tools, however, its value will be determined by the way it is put to use.

In looking ahead, there is one more characteristic of language that should be of increasing concern to our profession—its static quality. "Our language is a product of centuries, and most of our vocabulary reflects an older, pre-scientific view of the world. We retain a vocabulary suggestive of permanence when we know today that the only permanence is change. Metaphorically, we speak of 'the things of the world' as if they were like rocks, when we know they are more like flames. What we once thought were 'like nouns' now seem 'like verbs.'" [20]

Being sensitive to the fact that "a nonverbal world of process is represented in words that indicate a static quality" [21] is critical to our profession because we pride ourselves in being responsive to the changing needs of people. Paraphrasing Harkins, [22] we must understand that we're dealing with an emerging society. But when we allow our language to hold back the kinds of innovation that are needed to deal effectively with new social problems, how can we serve anybody except in terms of what our profession was set up to do for a society that's gone?

In planning for the future, we must retain our ability to make "semantic jumps," [23] to transcend the limitations of our existing language, to create new language in response to changing times. "The only way to make sense out of change is to plunge into it, move with it, and join the dance." [24] A worth ethic for parks, recreation, and tourism is but a first step.

Discussion Questions

1. What is the source of the discrepancy between the public's interpretation of the word "recreation" and the park, recreation, and tourism profession's? Can this discrepancy be eliminated?

2. How does labeling limit our perceptions? What are some resulting implications for people tagged with the following labels: playground leader, park ranger, recreation programmer, tour guide, therapeutic recreation specialist, outdoor recreation planner, person with a disability? Have you ever been victimized by labeling? How did it feel?

3. Why might the definitional problem with the word "recreation" act as a barrier to the advancement of the organized park, recreation, and tourism movement? What could be done about it?

4. How can the static quality of language inhibit the responsiveness of the park, recreation, and tourism profession to the changing needs of people?

5. How might the creation of new language (e.g., worth ethic) help extricate the park, recreation, and tourism profession from its linguistic predicament? Can you think of other language that could serve the profession similarly?

9

Creating Natural Resources

"We speak erroneously of 'artificial' materials, 'synthetics,' and so forth. The basis for this erroneous terminology is the notion that Nature has certain things which we call natural, and everything else is ['human-made'], ergo artificial. But what one learns in chemistry is that Nature wrote all the rules of structuring; [humans] do not invent chemical structuring rules; [we] only discover the rules. All the chemist can do is to find out what Nature permits, and any substances that are thus developed or discovered are inherently natural. It is very important to remember that."

—Buckminster Fuller

The lessons to be learned from a study of language extend beyond the realm of human interrelationships. They also have meaning for the way in which people relate to the natural environment. Park, recreation, and tourism professionals must be aware of these lessons also if we are to assume a leadership position in the campaign for responsible environmental stewardship. As William Brown charges in *Islands of Hope*, [1] no other profession is better suited for that position. Responsible environmental stewardship is, after all, our business. [2] The purpose of this chapter is to extend the discussion of language to environmental matters. In so doing, you will be presented with a somewhat different perspective on the environment and alerted to its possibilities in planning for the future. We hope this perspective will prove useful to you when engaging in barrier breaking of your own.

The Concept of a Natural Resource

Let us begin with the understanding that there is no such "thing" as a natural resource. There never has been and there never will be. That modern Western people behave as though there were is a result of many factors, not the least of which is our pattern of speech.

"We dissect nature along lines laid down by our native languages. The categories and types that we isolate from the world of phenomena we do not find there because they stare every observer in the face; on the contrary ... we cut nature up, organize it into concepts, and ascribe significances as we do, largely because we are parties to an agreement to organize it in this way—an agreement that holds throughout our speech community and is codified in our patterns of language." [3]

The idea that the day-to-day language we use influences the manner in which we come to know our environment is embodied in the principle of linguistic relativity. [4] Attributed to the work of Benjamin Whorf, linguistic relativity suggests that "the picture of the universe shifts from tongue to tongue." [5] And so it does.

In an essay entitled "Cultural Differences in the Interpretation of Natural Resources," [6] Alexander Spoehr contrasts the attitude of the Western world toward the environment with that of preliterate societies. He points out that Western people set themselves apart from nature and attempt to dominate it while preliterate people see themselves as a part of nature and therefore as being subservient to it.

Employing the logic of linguistic relativity, we can expect that these contrasting views of humankind's relationship to the environment are reflected in the language of their subscribers. Indeed they are. The term "natural resource," in particular, owes its existence to Western society's "ceaseless attempt at finding new and more intensive uses of nature." [7] In an effort to inventory those elements of the environment that are useful to us, we categorize or classify them as "natural resources." The environment itself tends to be considered only as a repository of matter which derives value when extracted for our use. Preliterate people, on the other hand, "lack the pervading instrumental attitude toward nature generally characteristic of [Western people]," [8] and lack the instrumental vocabulary as well.

That current Western thought "holds that habitat is something apart from [humans] and is to be manipulated to [our] advantage" [9] is manifested in other terms familiar to park, recreation, and tourism professionals such as "park administrator" and "land manager." This terminology is revealing because it connotes a separation between humans and nature. Moreover, it suggests an elevated status for humans in the conduct of worldly affairs. From this perspective, the environment is reduced to a prop, a backdrop for the human drama. The concept of linguistic relativity thus teaches that a natural resource is nothing more than a linguistic invention of the Western world. It is a mental sorting mechanism that has been developed to differentiate those elements of nature that are useful to us from those that are not. In this sense, the term "natural resource" is merely a reflection of an exploitive, homocentric view of the world. Yet, because it is embedded deeply in language, the idea of a natural resource is much more than this. It not only reflects the attitude of Western society toward the environment, it shapes it.

Reification of Natural Resources [10]

If Western people would accept the concept of a natural resource for what it is—a linguistic tool for organizing the elements of nature—there would be no problem. Unfortunately, we do otherwise. We reify natural resources. "The term 'reification' is used to describe the tendency to think that because there are certain words there must necessarily be certain 'things' that correspond to them. To reify is to 'thingify'." [11] Hence, because there are the words "natural resources" there must be certain "things" that correspond to them. Western people thus set out to look for those "things" that correspond to those words, and we are guided along the way by our existing interpretation of them.

Consider the consequences of reification by examining an important issue in parks, recreation, and tourism, the issue of limited resources. Historically, park, recreation, and tourism professionals have supported the cause of safeguarding those most pristine of "limited resources," the nation's wilderness areas. Through a series of legislative actions beginning with the establishment of the National Wilderness Preservation System in 1964, numerous tracts of land have been set aside as Wilderness. The 1964 Act calls for such tracts to fit the following specifications: "Wilderness is an area of undeveloped Federal land retaining its primeval character and influence, without permanent improvements of human habitation, which is protected and managed so as to preserve its natural condition and which (1) generally appears to have been affected primarily by the forces of nature, with the imprint of [human] work substantially unnoticeable; (2) has outstanding opportunities for solitude or a primitive and unconfined type of recreation; (3) has at least five thousand acres of land or is of sufficient size as to make practicable its preservation and use in an unimpaired condition; and (4) may also contain ecological, geological, or other features of scientific, educational, scenic, or historic value." [12] Utilizing this definition, recreation land policy makers have operationalized the concept of a wilderness resource. They have equated it with a physical entity. In effect, they have reified it. They have "thingified" it.

Given that land of the type described above is certainly in limited supply, we have been led by definition to believe that the wilderness resource also is so limited. Conservation organizations have thus resorted to a highly defensive posture in arguing for the preservation of those remaining few areas that qualify for Wilderness designation. In the heat of the debate, the distinction between the land and the label "wilderness" have been lost. They have been viewed as one.

Wilderness is not land, however. It is an abstraction, a quality that people ascribe to the landscape. [13] As such, it has the potential to be perceived in a variety of settings, [14] not just in those meeting the specifications of the Wilderness Act. Recognition of this is crucial for those who are charged with the responsibility of planning wilderness recreation opportunities because it means that the wilderness resource is not as limited as we have been led by our language to believe. Reification of wilderness not only shapes our thinking about its supply, it shapes our thinking about its appearance as well. Aldo Leopold recognized this when he lamented that "the Rocky Mountain system of wilderness covers a wide gamut of forest types, from the juniper breaks of the Southwest to the 'illimitable woods where rolls the Oregon.' It is lacking, however, in desert areas, probably because of that under-aged brand of esthetics which limits the definition of 'scenery' to lakes and pine trees." [15] In other words, since we "thingify" wilderness in the form of mountain wildlands, we tend to overlook other settings in which wilderness qualities also may be perceived.

In sum, reification of natural resources not only results in a narrow perspective on the present, it has a limiting effect on the range of alternatives to be considered in planning for the future. By equating natural resources with "things" and further qualifying them as being "limited," we limit our vision of what can be. We are not inclined to look in certain directions for solutions to planning problems because our language steers us away from them. So it is with the wilderness resource. So it is, no doubt, with others. If this power of language continues unabated, the future will not only be reflected in our speech, it will be shaped by it. We should never forget that.

Interpretation of Natural Resources

It should now be clear that there is no such thing as a natural resource. Neither is there a finite supply of natural resources fatefully awaiting the refining touch of the human hand. Rather, in all likelihood, there are enormous possibilities in terms of what environmental elements may be perceived as being useful to humankind.

As we have already learned, such perception is affected by language. There are other factors that also influence the interpretation of natural resources, and we should be equally conscious of them if we are serious about the idea of responsible environmental stewardship.

Technology

Whether or not something is perceived as being a natural resource depends to a considerable extent on existing technology. This relationship has been recognized in a variety of contexts familiar to park, recreation, and tourism professionals but nowhere has it been more evident than in the energy crisis of the 1970s. The reliance of American motorists on the automobile led to reduced mobility as oil supplies were cut back and as gasoline prices went up. [16] Remote recreational resources that once were readily accessible to the American public were now less so. If the energy crisis had worsened and the public remained dependent on its traditional means of transport, those areas would not have been interpreted as recreational resources much longer. How could they have been if they had become inaccessible?

Technology is not static, however. It changes. Western society's "singular bent toward technological invention" [17] guarantees it. Whether or not such change will ultimately result in increased or decreased mobility for the American public is a matter for debate; hence, whether or not a change in mobility will result in an increased or decreased "effective supply" [18] of recreational resources is also debatable. Yet existing technology will likely shape the direction of that change for the following reason: "A given technology, by making possible a particular kind of adaptation, tends to crystallize interest and knowledge around that segment of natural resources on which the technology depends." [19] Since Americans have grown accustomed to the convenience and comfort of automobiles, considerable energy is being expended to ensure that automobiles are kept rolling. Domestic oil exploration is being expanded. The mining of oil shale is being studied for its economic feasibility, gasification of coal is being examined, and so on. So it is that existing technology, not unlike existing language, predisposes us to search only in selected areas for relief from our problems. In this respect, an overdependence on current technology also has a significant limiting effect on our prospects for the future.

Social Structure

The interpretation of natural resources is also influenced by social structure. [20] This relationship has been graphically portrayed by Spoehr in a discussion of cross-cultural land ownership patterns. [21] The concepts of property rights and usufruct rights (renter's rights in legal parlance) are social conventions that have dramatically different implications for the way in which natural resources are treated. [22] The liberties afforded the holder of property rights far exceed those of the holder of usufruct rights. In the first instance, natural resources are viewed as commodities that are at the full disposal of their owners. In the second instance, natural resources are viewed as gifts that belong to another and that must be enjoyed in a way that does not destroy their substance.

In Western society, property rights are sacrosanct. Although one may disagree with the use to which the property of another is put, one has little legal or moral basis for registering a complaint. Pre-literate societies, on the other hand, understand Sigurd Olson when he proclaims, "Freedom gives no license to violate a heritage that belongs to the ages." [23] The prevailing social structure thus plays an important part in determining how natural resources are perceived by the members of a particular society. Parenthetically, it should not go unnoticed that while property rights are highly revered in the United States and therefore are deeply ingrained in the educational upbringing of its citizenry, those same citizens are expected to behave in usufruct fashion when partaking of its recreational resources. Without practice, these are indeed great expectations.

Habitat

Finally, there remains the issue of how people ultimately view their relationship to the world around them. Each person has a worldview, an epistemology, whether it is articulated or not. That view helps to shape behavior. It affects what a person feels should be done about conserving and developing habitat for human use. [24]

The predominant Western view of the world has already been described. It is an anthropocentric perspective that conceptually isolates natural resources as "that segment of the physical world that has a present or potential use for the survival and physical well-being of [humans], to be developed as far as possible through the application of scientific knowledge." [25] It is a view that has acted as a catalyst for many of the great scientific and technological accomplishments that now make life easier and more comfortable than it would have been otherwise.

The Western view of the world also is one that has contributed to the alienation of people from nature. It has led to the belief that nature exists for us, that nature derives its value only as a storehouse for our unrefined wares. Increasing urbanization and detachment from our "biological moorings" [26] are only reinforcing this homocentric view of the world. And while there are dissenting views (e.g., American Indian, eco-feminist, deep ecology perspectives), there are none that are more influential. For more than any other, the contemporary Western view of the world gives us license to act on the environment.

Human Resourcefulness

We have been discussing the major factors that influence humankind's interpretation of natural resources. As we have learned, language, technology, social structure, and perception of habitat serve collectively as a filter through which human impressions of the world pass. As these factors vary from culture to culture, so do the impressions of the world. It is in this sense that Jacob Bronowski tells us that "reality is not an exhibit for [our] inspection, labeled 'Do not touch.'" [27] Human impressions of nature are not exact copies of her. They are re-creations of her.

Bronowski's insight has important implications for park, recreation, and tourism professionals who are committed to the ideal of responsible environmental stewardship. It indicates that the predominant Western view of the world is neither an exact view nor the only possible view. It implies further that we have the power to make desirable changes in the Western view of the world by adjusting its filter. While the magnitude of this task far exceeds the capabilities of this book, perhaps we can at least contribute to the establishment of some appropriate points of departure.

Humankind's Creative Power

Let us start by paraphrasing the thoughts of Samuel Bois. [28] Because we humans take it for granted that natural resources are "out there" for us to see and theorize about, we miss the fact that their original singling out is an act of our own choice and creation. The choice may not be entirely personal or conscious, but it is our choice in the sense that we could, if we wanted, abstain from it or make a different choice. In other words, we human beings have the power to create natural resources through the exercise of our different choices.

Full appreciation of this creative power brings with it a series of revelations that have important implications for the way in which humankind ought to treat the environment. Foremost among them is the realization that all elements of nature have the potential to serve as resources for human enrichment. Their respective utility depends, of course, on fluctuations in the factors discussed previously. But as we shall see, those factors are subject to change. Consequently, if only for very selfish, homocentric reasons, it is prudent to treat the whole of nature with respect. Christopher Stone, although not happy with such an egotistical rationale for responsible environmental stewardship, concedes this point in *Should Trees Have Standing?* when he states that "one can say that we never know what is going to prove useful at some future time. In order to protect ourselves, therefore, we ought to be conservative now in our treatment of nature." [29]

A logical corollary to this revelation is that our power to create natural resources depends on the extent of our different choices which, in turn, depends on the extent of different environmental elements available to us. This succession of dependencies suggests a second selfish motive for responsible environmental stewardship— the preservation of our own creative power.

Humankind is thus presented with a very practical incentive for exercising restraint when acting on the environment. Such restraint differs in origin from that called for by Warren Johnson in *Muddling toward Frugality*, however, when he says, "We need the restraint provided by resource limitations." [30] While Johnson's statement is pejorative (i.e., it is prompted by concern over a reduction of natural resources), the present statement is meliorative (i.e., it is prompted by concern for an expansion of natural resources). [31] Thus, while Johnson's restraint is forced by increasingly limited choices brought about by diminishing environmental diversity, the restraint proposed here is voluntary and is based on the revelation that the more diversified the environment the more diversified the choices of the creators of natural resources.

Finally, whether we wish to face up to it or not, the power to create natural resources carries with it responsibility for the future. The philosopher, Oliver Reiser, has characterized this responsibility in the following two axioms: "Not one of us is without the power to contribute to the making of the future. Not one of us is free from responsibility for making the future." [32] We cannot shirk from this responsibility. It is ours alone. The future is open-ended. It will become what we allow it to become. It's as simple, and as complex, as that.

Adjusting the Filter

The late British economist, E. F. Schumacher, summarized the task of our generation as one of "metaphysical reconstruction." [33] He argued that we humans must adopt a more sensitive and caring attitude toward each other and toward the environment that supports us if we are to enjoy continued prosperity on this planet. Let's apply what we have learned in this chapter to this reconstruction process by touching briefly upon some possibilities for language, technology, social structure, and perception of habitat.

Language

Reiser reminds us of the difficulty inherent in changing our thinking about the world as long as we are shackled to our existing language. "We must remember that we still have before us the problem of what may be called the language-centric predicament, namely, that we must use language to think and talk about language."[34] In other words, since we think in language, we must change our language to change our thinking. The language-centric predicament leads to the domain of creative semantics. Creative semantics deals with what words ought to mean in a reconstructed society. [35] Creative semantics works in two ways. First, it reinterprets old symbols for use in novel circumstances. Second, it creates new symbols for a new world with its new language. [36] We have already employed creative semantics in its second sense in our development of a worth ethic for parks, recreation, and tourism. Creative semantics can be equally useful when employed in its first sense. Consider, for example, the replacement of the terms "park administrator" and "land manager" with the terms "park steward" and "land custodian." Are there not fundamentally different connotations associated with the latter terms? Do they not suggest a respectful, responsible, and related attitude toward the environment that is absent in the former terms? Are they not a more accurate reflection of your feelings about the environment of which you are a principal caretaker? Are you not, after all, a steward of access, a custodian of choice? Reconstruct your language. And remember, while it may seem like a very small beginning, "a change in language can transform our appreciation of the Cosmos." [37]

Technology

Employing language-centric logic, if we initiate changes in our speaking of the kind suggested above, we can expect parallel changes in our thinking. Changes in our thinking will then surface in the form of new values governing our relationship to the environment.

This logic has major implications for technology because humankind's basic way of relating to the environment is technological. That is, technology is the means by which we humans adapt to the environment. If we truly embrace a more caring and sensitive attitude toward nature, our value system will not allow us to use technology in uncaring or insensitive ways. So it is that Schumacher speaks of working toward "technology with a human face" [38] and Johnson calls for "winning technologies" [39] based on responsible stewardship of renewable resources bequeathed to us by the sun, land, wind, and water. Technology is not inherently good or bad. Neither is it necessarily a dehumanizing force. Technology is a tool that exists to serve our ends. If you object to the nature of a particular technology, reassess the ends for which that technology has been developed. In the final analysis, "the values existing at any given time will determine the technological choices that a society will make." [40]

Social Structure

Just as a society's technological choices are governed by its prevailing set of values, so too is the nature of its social structure. "Cultures are, in the final analysis, value-guided systems." [41] Value changes brought about by the reconstruction of language and thought processes can be expected to precipitate similar changes in social processes.

Evidence of social change suggesting that the Western world is moving toward a more caring and sensitive attitude toward the environment is emerging, albeit slowly. For example, results of the Stanford Research Institute's Values and Lifestyles Program [42] indicate a shift in consumerism which reflects a less materialistic orientation to life. A growing percentage of the American buying public is becoming inwardly directed and environmentally aware. Should this pattern continue to unfold, the era of conspicuous consumption may give way to an era of materialistic frugality based on our society's maturing ecological conscience.

Further proof of shifting Western values is reflected in the increasing attention being paid to the idea of legal rights for natural objects. [43] While the extension of a social conscience from people to land is not a novel concept, [44] the seriousness with which the concept is being examined in contemporary legal circles is novel. First evidenced in the rationale for establishing the National Environmental Policy Act of 1969, [45] the concern for the rights of natural objects has grown dramatically in recent years. This concern has been manifested in heated debates over the management of endangered species habitats as well as in debates over the management of outdoor recreation environments. The fact that there even are such debates suggests changing values in the Western world.

We cannot expect rapid transformations in our social structure in response to a new set of environmental values. The acceptance of any new value system necessitates letting go of the established one. This is hard giving up indeed. It means forsaking what is familiar and time tested for what is unfamiliar and untested. At the same time, we must remember that a society, not unlike its individual members, must adapt itself to the changing conditions of its environment if it is to survive. To paraphrase the systems scientist, Ervin Laszlo, [46] societies must be able to evolve new structures and new functions. They must be able to create themselves in time.

Perceptions of Habitat

There are at least two ways of thinking about the part that humankind will play in creating future societies. First, it is possible that we will actually design them in some premeditated fashion. Whether by consensus or by fiat, if we human beings put our minds to it, we have the power to create and carry out plans that can shape the form and meaning of tomorrow's world. Second, it is possible that the future will assume its identity largely by accident. This possibility stems both from the fact that we do not have control over all the factors that may contribute to the shaping of the future and the fact that we frequently act on incomplete knowledge, that we make mistakes, and that we cannot foresee all the possible consequences of our present actions.

Underpinning these two divergent prospects are two equally divergent principles of human workmanship: the principle of design and the principle of eolithism. [47, 48] Both principles deserve attention because they have quite different implications for the way in which we will look after our habitat.

Central to the principle of design is the idea that the craftsperson knows what she or he wants. [49] One doesn't set out to build something, whether it is a utensil or a utopia, unless one has a good idea of what that something is to look like. Equipped with a goal, the designer's task becomes one of deciding how best to reach it. The design process necessitates familiarity with suitable building materials and knowledge of their degree of uniformity for mass production purposes. Eventually, after the design has been applied to the material in the thought construction process, the material is applied to the design in the physical construction process. Upon completion, the structure can be evaluated in light of its intended purpose.

A distinguishing feature of the principle of design is that once a goal is established, all subsequent decisions become instrumental to reaching that goal. [50] Decisions about the relative value of building materials, for example, are made in terms of their goodness of fit to the specifications of the overall design goal. The goal itself tends not to come under scrutiny. So it is with the goal of production in the industrial world. "There is disagreement as to which mode of production is the truly good one, not whether production defines the nature of human good." [51]

Those who embrace the principle of design thus operate from a rather limited perspective. As David Hawkins observes, "the essential limitations of the principle of design lie in the givenness and fixity of goals, and the need to eliminate variety and heterogeneity from the means and materials; they are thereby reduced in any significance or value they may have, except in serving those given ends." [52] Drawing on the previous example, those elements of nature that do not serve the prevailing industrial goal of production are thereby reduced in any significance or value they may have. This explains in part the difficulty of mustering public support for the continuing development and maintenance of outdoor recreation environments at a time when increasing industrial productivity is the predominant national concern. It is just not very clear how park and recreation settings contribute to that productivity.

In contrast to the principle of design is the principle of eolithism. "An eolith is literally a piece of junk remaining from the Stone Age."[53] It refers to something that is accidentally discovered, something that is already suited to a given end and strongly suggestive of that end. The classic example is a stone resting in a primeval field, weathered to a form suitable for a spearhead. Its discoverer, perhaps tripping over it, has never even considered the concept of a spear, let alone a spearhead. It is only through a serendipitous occurrence, the act of tripping and falling over the stone, that the eolith is brought to the attention of its discoverer and considered for its possible utility.

Fashioners of eoliths differ markedly from designers in their attitude toward the surrounding environment. While designers know what they want and what materials are required, eolithic craftspersons do not. They keep an open mind about the ends they are to pursue as well as their materials. They are collectors of things that others (designers) have discarded. They know such materials may serve purposes that have yet to be defined or even conceptualized. They respect those materials for their potential as well as their present value. Eolithic craftspersons are, in the final analysis, like a junkman.

Junkmen, as you know, do not occupy a position of high regard in the Western world. It is the designers who are lauded for their carefully laid out plans and attention to detail. But one has to wonder if this praise is not misplaced. With respect to fostering responsible environmental stewardship, is it not the fashioners of eoliths who exhibit a more caring and sensitive attitude toward the whole of nature? Is this not because eolithic craftspersons recognize that nature provides countless possibilities for enriching human welfare, and that those possibilities must be nurtured in perpetuity? Is it not, then, the principle of eolithism that ought to serve as our guide when interacting with the Earth?

Being About Your Business

In his thoughtful book *Reflections from the North Country*, Sigurd Olson remarks that "the greatest achievement of our flight to the moon is the picture of the earth, a living blue-green planet whirling in the dark endless void of space, and the realization that this is home." [54] What greater responsibility could a profession have than to be entrusted with the stewardship of that home's most treasured furnishings?

Hopefully, this chapter has equipped you with a perspective that will prove useful in carrying out your custodial duties. Now, at last, liberated from the bounds of language, technology, social structure, and perception of habitat, you are free to lead the crusade for responsible environmental stewardship, and to learn from a junkman.

Discussion Questions

1. How can the reification of recreation resources narrow the recreation planning perspective? What can be done about it?
2. How do technology, social structure, and the perception of habitat influence the interpretation of natural resources?
3. In what way can human beings create natural resources? What does this power imply in terms of our responsibility for the future?
4. Why is responsible environmental stewardship sensible even from a selfish, homocentric perspective?
5. How do eolithic craftspersons differ from designers in their orientation to life? What are the strengths and weaknesses of each perspective in planning for the future? Which perspective appeals to you more? Why?

10

Reaching for a Higher Education

"We are nature seeing nature."

—Susan Griffin

The kind of learning emphasized in this book requires more than being receptive to new ideas. It requires a propensity to seek them out as well. This "need to know" in turn demands going beyond the bounds of traditional educational inquiry. It demands rising above the limited perspectives of academic specializations in the search for a broader and more integrated understanding of the world.

Jere Clark captures the essence of this educational challenge in describing the preferred nature of today's students: "[Students] must be viewed as . . . potentially self-propelled, self-guided navigators moving not only through the relatively familiar, static, and simple terrain of today but also into the relatively strange, dynamic, interdependent and complex world of tomorrow. [Their] minds must be programmed so that [they] can reprogram [them] whenever necessary throughout [their] lifetimes." [1]

Clark's description is as apt for park, recreation, and tourism students as it is for any other professionals of the future. They too will be living in a world characterized by dynamism, interdependence, and increasing complexity. They too will be challenged to steer their way through a constantly changing terrain. Consequently, they too must be programmed so that they can reprogram themselves whenever necessary throughout their lifetimes.

The task of this chapter is to define the nature of the programming that must take place in the minds of today's park, recreation, and tourism students if they are to become self-propelled, self-guided navigators of tomorrow.

The Crisis of Accountability

The task begins with a caveat. There is a crisis confronting park, recreation, and tourism education today, a crisis of accountability. Faced with the reality of increasingly limited resources, college and university administrators are demanding that educators document their reason for being, that they prove their worth to higher education in times of fiscal austerity and retrenchment.

The response of park, recreation, and tourism educators to the crisis of accountability has commonly been rooted in claims of academic professionalism. Efforts to generate and define a body of knowledge unique to the park, recreation, and tourism field, [2] to transmit that knowledge to students through a sequence of academically rigorous core courses, [3] and to develop high standards of professional preparation to ensure quality control in the production of graduates, [4] all have been pursued vigorously by academicians in our field in their struggle for acceptance. Whether such efforts will see them through the fiscally imposed crisis of accountability is not clear. What is clear is that by clinging to the traditional model of academic professionalism, park, recreation, and tourism educators inadvertently are laying the foundation for a much more severe crisis, a crisis of relevance. [5]

Limits of Academic Professionalism

"The history of higher education since the latter part of the nineteenth century has been the history of the rise to dominance of the academic profession and of the university as its principal institutional expression." [6] The number of academic disciplines and departments has grown tremendously in response to the conviction that a complex world can best be understood by reducing it to its component parts and then studying those parts in detail. That conviction has been reinforced by the fact that individuals are limited in their capacity to process information. Researchers and educators alike have thus been encouraged to study one thing in great depth and then through cooperative efforts to piece together the lessons of those inquiries to explain larger processes. As the general systems philosopher Ervin Laszlo states, "this is the ideal of specialization, and it has led to the great advances in the sciences and technologies that now affect the lives of us all." [7]

Academic professionalism has not been without its problems, however. Among them has been the tendency for disciplines to isolate themselves in their rigorous pursuit of specialized knowledge. Roderick Nash illustrates the consequences of this atomistic orientation for the academician in a brief autobiographical sketch:

> In high school, I was simply a student, but soon after entering college, advisers urged me to think about focusing my attention on either the humanities, social studies, or sciences. Later I was obliged to choose a major: history. By my senior year, "history" became "American history." At the master's level, I concentrated on American social and intellectual history, but my Ph.D. dissertation involved a small corner of that field: American attitudes toward national parks and wilderness. Further specialization found me studying Yosemite National Park, then one part of it (the Hetch Hetchy Valley where a dam was constructed), and finally the history of the Hetch Hetchy controversy between 1908 and 1913! At this point, the profession deemed my research worthy of publication. I was a big fish in a very, very small pond. Six years of effort had brought me to a position where I could talk about my subject to hardly anyone except myself. [8]

Nash's testimony reflects a major difficulty with contemporary higher education. The equation of professionalism with specialization creates an intellectual environment in which narrow and highly technical thinking is encouraged, while broad and highly integrative thinking is discouraged. Discipline specific jargon, academic territorialism, and other barriers to communication only serve to intensify that environment. Consequently, "knowledge, instead of being pursued in depth and integrated in breadth, is pursued in depth in relative isolation." [9]

Beyond this communication problem, however, is the fact that academic professionalism is limited in its ability to contribute to the resolution of many pressing social issues. While specialized knowledge is quite useful in detailing relatively simple causal or correlative relationships, it is not well suited for explaining "how a number of different things act together when exposed to a number of different influences at the same time. And almost everything we encounter around us contains a large number of different things and is exposed to a number of different influences." [10]

In sum, a tradition of atomistic inquiry and increasing specialization, while yielding a substantial amount of isolated bits and pieces of knowledge, has failed to provide a synthesizing view of the world. The need for that synthesis is evident in times when international communities are becoming increasingly interdependent and international problems are becoming increasingly interconnected.

It is indeed ironic that park, recreation, and tourism educators find it necessary to justify their existence in higher education in terms of academic professionalism when the limits of that intellectual orientation are being widely acknowledged. Yet that is the case. As Bernard Mead noted, "the professional preparation programs … look to specialization and exclusion instead of commonalty and unification." [11] "Programs have evolved from specialization in public and volunteer recreation services to a wide-range of specializations which include resource management; environmental interpretation; park law enforcement; therapeutic recreation; park planning; leisure counseling; leisure education; commercial recreation; outdoor education; and a myriad of other occupational specializations." [12] When one adds "tourism" to this long list of specializations, one might ask, "Where will it end?" If, "as the story has it, that a geologist specializing in soft rocks finds himself a lonely man in a congress on hard-rock geology," [13] is the individual specializing in therapeutic recreation destined to find herself a lonely person in a congress on recreation therapy? Is there not a danger in such specialization of park, recreation, and tourism's subareas creating their own barriers and closed bubbles of knowledge? Is there not also a danger of park, recreation, and tourism's educators losing touch with each other and with the very essence of their field in the search for academic respectability? [14] Is there not, then, an ultimate danger of park, recreation, and tourism education becoming irrelevant?

Rethinking Park, Recreation, and Tourism Education

In an insightful essay entitled "Logs, Universities, and the Environmental Education Compromise," [15] Roderick Nash speaks of environmental education as a multidisciplinary process that draws upon a variety of disciplines to resolve existing environmental problems. He defends the value of environmental education not in terms of academic professionalism but in terms of its relevance as a synthesizing field of study.

There is a parallel between environmental education and park, recreation, and tourism education. Consider the following observation by Douglas Sessoms:

> The literature of the recreation and park profession is built upon the findings and practices of a wide range of related occupations and specialties. For example, park managers depend heavily upon the work of biologists, naturalists, landscape architects, and foresters. Programmers turn to physical education, art, music, and other performing fields for instruction in activity skill development. Supervisors and program developers would be laboring under heavy odds if it were not for methods and concepts they have adapted from social work and social psychology. The field's administrative literature mirrors the writings of public and business administration; their concepts and discoveries are used to expedite the recreation and park delivery system. And finally, it is the sociologists, psychologists, and economists who supply the field's theoretical and research underpinnings. [16]

Just as environmental education relies on the expertise of other disciplines to deal with environmental problems, so does park, recreation, and tourism education rely on the expertise of other disciplines to deal with problems related to leisure. Just as the specialty of environmental education is synthesis, so too is synthesis the specialty of park, recreation, and tourism education.

Park, recreation, and tourism educators need not be apologetic for the multidisciplinary nature of our field of study. On the contrary, the birth of the ecology movement, the subsequent growth of environmental studies, the resurgence of general education, and in particular the rise of general systems philosophy, all may be viewed as reactions to the shortcomings of academic professionalism.

They reflect a need for interdisciplinary approaches to increasingly complex physical and social problems. They are integrative fields of study. They represent the academic hope for the future.

Defusing the Crisis of Relevance

B. L. Driver, a former researcher with the United States Forest Service, observed that "educational and research institutions tend to organize themselves into disciplines. The real world tends to carve itself up into problems. Sometimes the two are coincident; most frequently they are not." [17] To defuse the crisis of relevance, educators in our field must close the gap described by Driver. They must realize, as Peter Drucker argues, [18] that "we are shifting from a Cartesian view of the universe, in which the accent has been on parts and elements, to a configuration view, with the emphasis on wholes and patterns," and that this shift "challenges every single dividing line between areas of study and knowledge." They must realize further that "the real need of the day is to restructure knowledge into simple, integrated, and flexible patterns which are broadly applicable to wide ranges of phenomena." [19] To meet this need, the intellectual navigator of tomorrow must be equipped with a "simple interdisciplinary model that will help determine what information [she or] he requires in virtually any situation, and serve as a framework for organizing and using that information." [20]

Contemporary general systems theory [21] offers promise as such a model. Developed as a theoretical framework for assessing organizational similarities among systems of all kinds, general systems theory focuses on organizational structure rather than organizational content in the search for understanding. Recognizing that changing content is the natural order of things, [22] attention is directed toward the identification of "invariances of organization"[23] that may be useful for explaining how things work across systems over time.

The utility of the general systems orientation is reflected vividly in John Crompton's article "A Recreation System Model" published in *Leisure Sciences*. [24] Crompton applies his understanding of the basic managerial functions of systems—what he terms planning, execution, and control—to the specific case of a public recreation department. Through a detailing of his model he then describes how such a department carries out its managerial functions in a five-stage sequence—what he refers to as input, process, output, transposition, and outcome. Finally, he emphasizes the importance of understanding the interrelationships among the five stages and their coordination to ensure desired outcomes for recreationists.

What allows Crompton to treat a public recreation department as if it were like any other management system? It is the assumption that while content may vary from system to system, the organizational properties remain the same across systems. By focusing on those shared aspects of organization, he is thus able to offer insights about a recreation management system based on his understanding of the organizational properties of systems in general.

Crompton's article also serves to underscore the importance of general systems theory as a unifying language for problem solvers. His discussion of the evaluative role of feedback mechanisms in the outcome stage of his recreation system model, for example, is a specific application of terminology that is generally understood across disciplines. It is language that is associated with barrier breaking of the most significant kind.

Properly schooled in the basic tenets of general systems theory, it therefore seems reasonable to expect that today's park, recreation, and tourism students would be equipped similarly with reliable navigational tools for steering their way through a future of constantly changing content.

Reaching for a Higher Education

"That's fine," say the park, recreation, and tourism educators among you, "but what do I do on Monday morning? [25] How can I actually incorporate the precepts of general systems thinking into my day-to-day teaching?"

The following three proposals are offered to assist park, recreation, and tourism educators in the initial stages of that process. Their implementation should contribute toward what Kenneth Boulding calls the "indispensable minimum of knowledge" [26] required to enable students to program their own minds in such a way that they will be able to reprogram themselves whenever necessary throughout their lifetimes.

1. Park, recreation, and tourism educators must adapt their curricular offerings to the reality that subject matters are interrelated. As Mead suggested, this means the "reorientation of preparation programs from job-oriented skills and knowledge to basic conceptual issues and knowledge areas which have broad range application." [27] This requires concentrating on the generation of an "optimum blend of such problem-solving skills as the ability to observe (especially to recognize patterns), communicate, value, imagine, reason, hypothesize, measure, model, select, plan, test, implement, and re-evaluate." [28] These are the navigational tools of tomorrow. They must be honed in the classroom of today.

2. Park, recreation, and tourism educators must foster communication in a common language across disciplines. In their search for the commonality that unites disciplines, as opposed to a preoccupation with differences that tend to separate them, park, recreation, and tourism educators must cultivate the ability to speak in an integrative manner. This requires becoming fluent in the language of general systems that has been developed to break down barriers associated with academic professionalism.

3. Finally, park, recreation, and tourism educators must produce graduates who, although they may be specialists, have generalized ears. [29] Paraphrasing Nash, it is important that park, recreation, and tourism students know what questions to ask and to whom to direct them. They also must know how to interpret the answers and fit them into the jigsaw puzzle of leisure problem-solving. This requires nurturing students' transpective ability, the ability to compare critically different ways of thought, and to incorporate the lessons of those comparisons into their own ever-expanding pattern of comprehension. [30]

In his book *Toward a Theory of Instruction*, [31] Jerome Bruner calls for the development of "metaskills" and a "metalanguage" to help people adjust to a world in flux. This chapter has suggested that general systems theory serves both purposes. In addition to its utility as an organizing structure or mental scaffolding for conceptualizations, it is a vocabulary for communicating across disciplines.[32] It is both a way of viewing the world and a way of talking about the world. To succeed as self-propelled, self-guided professionals of tomorrow, it is becoming increasingly apparent that today's park, recreation, and tourism students must avail themselves of the insights afforded by both perspectives

Discussion Questions

1. Why might the traditional orientation to learning be ill-suited for understanding increasingly complex social problems? How might a systems view of the world enhance such understanding?
2. How might the equation of professionalism with academic specialization lead to irrelevance in park, recreation, and tourism education? Do you agree or disagree with this line of reasoning? Explain your thinking.
3. Discuss the pros and cons of accreditation of park, recreation, and tourism curricula in colleges and universities in light of the theme of this chapter.
4. Contrast the problem-solving skills emphasized on these pages with the traditional job-oriented skills emphasized in many professional preparation programs. Which skills seem more relevant to you in a world of rapid change?
5. What do you believe will be the necessary navigational tools for tomorrow's park, recreation, and tourism professionals? Are you being, or have you been, equipped adequately for that future? What changes in academic programming would you recommend based on your experience? Are you confident of your abilities as a self-propelled, self-guided navigator? Discuss your feelings.

11

Serving the Human Potential

"Self-fulfillment ... is the end of human purposeful behavior."

—Ervin Laszlo

Imagine that the end of the world is at hand. Imagine further that the same technological know-how that has equipped human-kind with its frightening capacity for self-destruction has afforded it one more opportunity to start anew—on another planet not unlike the Earth in its pristine state. Twelve individuals have been selected by occupation to plant the seeds of that new beginning. They are a farmer, musician, educator, physician, carpenter, novelist, child-rearer, minister, poet, scientist, organizer/leader, and actor. Each has been chosen for possessing the highest level of expertise in his or her respective field.

Now envision the 12 survivors hurtling through space, saddened by the demise of their homeland but at the same time buoyed by the prospect of a fresh start. Once again, however, the technology that "let them down" on Earth deals a cruel blow. Alas, there is only enough oxygen on board to ensure that one-half of the passengers reach their destination. Six must go out the hatch. There is no other choice. Now who will they be?

Over the years that the authors have been employing this values clarification exercise, the results have remained remarkably consistent. While there are predictable testimonials to the importance of musicians, novelists, poets, and actors in enhancing the quality of human life, they are dispatched with quickly. More serious debate ensues over the fate of the child-rearer, educator, minister, and organizer/leader. Which two are destined for the hatch varies, in fact, from exercise to exercise. Without question, though, the farmer, physician, carpenter, and scientist are retained—usually in that order.

In discussing the exercise, participants are asked to recall the criterion that served as a basis for their decisions. Inevitably their remarks boil down to a concern for survival. The farmer, physician, carpenter, and scientist are best equipped to provide the basic necessities of life. Unless those needs are met, the settlers of the imaginary new frontier will have little need for the contributions of a musician, novelist, poet, or actor. Survival first, quality of survival second. It's as simple as that.

By this time, someone will have brought up Abraham Maslow's hierarchy of human needs. [1] The exercise, it is avowed, confirms the logic of the pyramid. Until the lower order physiological and safety needs are satisfied, humankind does not pay much attention to the higher order needs for love and belongingness, self-esteem, and self-actualization. "To be sure," the participants agree, "lofty ideals are not easy to pursue on an empty stomach." [2]

At this point, a connection is called for between the lesson of the exercise and public concern for park, recreation, and tourism services. "Easy," they say. Parks, recreation, and tourism impact the quality of human life, not its survival. In times of plenty, citizens can afford to be concerned about the delivery of these services. In hard times they cannot. It's a matter of priorities.

Parks, recreation, and tourism as frosting. Once again, it's a perspective all too familiar to those of us who devote our careers to the ideals of this field—a perspective that is confronted on a daily basis. But until now, at least, some comfort could be taken in the thought that this was the perspective only of the unaware, the uneducated. Park, recreation, and tourism people knew better. If only at an intuitive level, we understood that we were making a significant contribution to the very survival of humanity. Until now. Until this exercise. Now we too found ourselves saying that parks, recreation, and tourism were somehow secondary in importance.

Typically, participants leave the exercise disillusioned, having second thoughts about their career choice. That's okay. Their spirits will be uplifted at the next meeting when they find out how mistaken their priorities really are.

Survival or Quality of Survival? [3]

Who can argue against survival as the summum bonum, the ultimate goal for humankind? Do we not all harbor thoughts of immortality, thoughts of escaping the inevitability of the aging process? Do we not take quiet delight in reading about scientific breakthroughs that suggest the possibility of extending the human life span? Organ transplants. The implications of recombinant DNA research. Cloning. Where will it end? Must it end? Will science come through? Is human transcendence possible?

Perhaps we can learn from the work of Leonard Hayflick. Hayflick, a cell biologist, studied the aging process of normal cells from human lung tissue maintained in a culture in vitro (outside the body). [4] Allowed to prosper and multiply, the cells doubled rapidly at first but then over time diminished in their doubling capacity. Eventually, the cells failed to multiply at all and died. Through a series of such experiments, Hayflick and others have concluded that the human aging process may be genetically predetermined. [5] That is, it appears that individual human beings are programmed at birth to fail. While the exact timing of that failure is subject to some variation within the human species, it is ultimately unavoidable. Much like your favorite car, "barring total replacement of all vital elements, deterioration is inevitable." [6]

If Hayflick's conclusion is correct, then the issue of survival, at least in an individual sense, loses much of its luster. If survival, if immortality, is out of the question, then of much more importance to each human being is the issue of how to make the most out of the time one has. And that is a question of quality.

"Yes," you say, "but you are talking about survival in the long run. In the short run, it's a different story. One must still solve the problem of getting through today, even if one prefers to concentrate on the problem of how to build a better tomorrow. Anyone who has lived through the Great Depression recognizes this. In a fundamental sense, one must always be concerned about survival first."

So it is that humankind, in the name of survival, stands ready to take whatever action seems necessary to ensure its continuation. If, on occasion, that means relegating issues related to the quality of human life to the back burner, so be it. If clean air and water must be sacrificed for the sake of economic prosperity, for the sake of jobs, food on the table, and clothing and shelter for the family, so be it. In time, perhaps if it becomes more affordable, the air and water can be cleansed, greater care can be given to the design of healthier living environments, and park and recreation services can be restored. If not, at least humankind will have survived.

Clearly, there is something wrong with this line of thinking.

The Issue of Ends and Means

Survival, by itself, is not a sufficient description of a desirable end state for humanity. [7] It offers no guidelines for fulfillment. As David Hawkins points out, "such a goal only appears to govern, in the minds of those who claim it as their guide, because they have unwittingly read into it some dominant bias which is, in fact, highly specific—the projection of their own highly specific commitments and engrossments written large." [8] So it is that both pro and anti-nuclear power advocates make their claims in the name of survival. So it is also that both utilitarian and preservationist interests make their claims for wilderness. Who's to say who is right?

Survival as the summum bonum for humankind must be defined in a way that includes a description of its preferred nature as well. In other words, there is little point in talking about survival without also talking about the quality of survival. The end cannot be conceived independently of its means. [9] Survival is not an either-or proposition. It is a matter of kind. To overlook this fact is to commit the human race to a path of self-dissolution in the name of survival alone. While there may be ample life along such a path, there will be very little in the way of humanness. And while there may even be immortality, it will more than likely be confined to a petri dish.

The Human Potential

To speak of the human potential is to speak of more than the chances for mere survival. To speak of the human potential is to speak of the chances for enriching the quality of human life as well. Ends and means. They are inseparable issues. They are one.

What is the nature of the human potential? Can it be reached? Where do park, recreation, and tourism professionals fit in? Let's begin to address these questions with a brief look at the raw materials.

Hardware and Software [10]

There are really only two kinds of things in this world. First, there are the things you can touch, taste, smell, hear, and see; things like tables and chairs, paper and pencils, hot dogs and hamburgers, cats and dogs, and so on. These things are called "hardware." Of all the hardware on Earth, one set stands out in terms of its intricacy, complexity, integrated functions, and careful construction. It is the human body.

Second, there are the things you cannot touch, taste, smell, hear, or see; things like emotions, ideas, thoughts, and feelings. These things are called "software." Of all the software on Earth, one set also stands out in terms of its intricacy, complexity, integrated functions, and careful construction. It is the human mind.

The convergence of the human body with the human mind to form a human being represents the most sophisticated and marvelous combination of hardware and software imaginable. It is truly a union to be celebrated, nurtured, and encouraged to its fullest potential. Therein, as with all professions, lies the mission of parks, recreation, and tourism. In the name of human fulfillment, park, recreation, and tourism professionals are obliged to "[act] on the environment, both the internal one of the organism and the external one of the society, and [make] it compatible with the expression of one's potentials."[11] That ideal, that state of compatibility, is the preferred nature of human survival. That is the summum bonum to which our profession ought to aspire.

Duality of the Human Condition

Note the delicate balance that is called for. Park, recreation, and tourism professionals are charged to act on both the individual and society in ways that will make them compatible with the expression of the human potential. It stands to reason, therefore, that this state of compatibility demands certain concessions from both the individual and the larger society to which the individual belongs. Just what those concessions entail will be discussed shortly. For now, however, recognize that they reflect the dualistic nature of human beings. As Ervin Laszlo notes, "physiologically [a human being] is an individual whole, whereas sociologically he [or she] is an integrated (or a recalcitrant) part. And since [humans] are endowed with consciousness, psychologically [we] are both whole and part—a duality which, when not recognized..., can lead to confusion and distress." [12] Consequently, when one talks of serving the human potential, when one talks of human fulfillment, one is talking about the possibilities for humankind both as biological and sociocultural beings. One is talking about trying to promote bodily as well as mental health. One is talking about maximizing what is right for both the human hardware and the human software in unity. In sum, one is talking about a most delicate balance indeed.

Serving the Human Potential

Can the human potential be reached? As discussed earlier in this book, there are no assurances. It is largely a personal matter, an issue to be addressed by each individual. What can be assured, however, is that the environment in which we human beings live is made as conducive as possible to our full growth and development. And that is where park, recreation, and tourism professionals fit in.

By embracing the three tenets of the worth ethic—respect as a birthright, freedom to grow, and opportunities for choice—and championing them to the citizenry in the name of human fulfillment, our profession can contribute to the creation of an environment that nourishes the human potential. We, as much as any farmer, physician, carpenter, or scientist, can play a vital role in orchestrating an atmosphere of hope for humankind. We can serve as principal architects of a new beginning on this planet.

No doubt we have our work cut out for us. The field of parks, recreation, and tourism is, in many respects, a "maternalistic" one that is attempting to exist in what many would claim to be a "paternalistic" world. To the extent that leisure "mothering" is effective in changing behavior (e.g., combating social deviance, leading people toward healthy lifestyles, promoting minimum impact philosophy), we are likely to garner support for the provision of our services. But make no mistake about it, to be guided in the delivery of those services by a worth ethic that is fundamentally an ethic of caring, to advocate "soft" qualities in what many perceive to be a world of "hard" realities, is to be at odds with much of what drives contemporary American life. [13, 14] Nevertheless, we believe there is no professional body better suited for the undertaking. It is now time to get on with it. We must gear up psychologically for the task at hand, and then, as J. B. Nash so aptly put it, "travel hopefully." [15]

Guidelines for Action

To assist you along the way, we have compiled the following general guidelines for action. They are not intended to dictate your behavior. Rather, they are offered as conceptual shoulders to lean on when confronting specific problems in the administration of your duties.

1. "Fulfillment is predicated upon the freedom to become what one is capable of being—that is upon the functional autonomy of human beings in society. [16] Park, recreation, and tourism professionals should be committed to the ideal of individual freedom. We should act on the environment, both the internal one of the organism and the external one of society, and make it compatible with the expression of that freedom. [17] This means that society must make a concession to its members. It must give them room to grow and develop, to succeed and fail, to express their initiative, creativity, and fulfillment as individual human beings. This also means that the individual must make a concession to society. One must accept responsibility for one's behavior.

2. In matters of preference, [18] park, recreation, and tourism professionals should yield to the individual. The park, recreation, and tourism profession should be committed to the ideal of expanding opportunities for choice. Although some of the opportunities desired by the public may conflict with values held by those of us charged with supplying them, [19] the opportunities should be made available as long as they are socially acceptable.

To do otherwise is to impinge upon individual freedom and to reduce the possibilities for human fulfillment.

3. In matters of principle, [20] park, recreation, and tourism professionals should yield to society. On occasion, matters of personal preference clash with matters of social principle. That is, sometimes a preference one has as an individual conflicts with a preference one has as a member of society. On a personal level, for example, one may wish to feed the bear. On a social level, however, one recognizes the negative effects of such behavior on both the future of the bear and the future quality of visits to the bear's habitat by other citizens. [21] In those instances, park, recreation, and tourism professionals should support the social principle governing the situation. To do otherwise is to absolve individuals from responsibility for their behavior.

4. "Examine each question in terms of what is ethically and esthetically right, as well as what is economically expedient. A thing is right when it intends to preserve the integrity, stability, and beauty of the biotic community. It is wrong when it tends otherwise." [22] The interplay between one's freedom to act and one's responsibility to society for one's actions is necessarily "bounded by the limits of compatibility with the dynamic structure of the whole." [23] One's behavior must be in accordance not only with the welfare of humankind, but also with the welfare of the larger community of life. To do otherwise is to jeopardize not only individual freedom and human fulfillment, but ultimately to jeopardize the existence of humanity itself.

In the final analysis, there may be no demonstrable evidence to suggest the park, recreation, and tourism profession's indispensability to the survival of life on Earth. But there is every reason to believe this profession is indispensable to the quality of that life. In this sense, park, recreation, and tourism professionals do indeed contribute to the very survival of humanity, and for this reason we had best roll up our sleeves and get down to work.

Discussion Questions

1. Why is survival insufficient as a description of a desirable end state for humankind? What is missing?
2. Relate survival and quality of survival to the issue of ends and means. Why should they be thought of as inseparable?
3. What is the role of the park, recreation, and tourism profession in serving the human potential?
4. When should park, recreation, and tourism professionals accommodate individual preferences? When should we bow to social principles? Can you think of any recreational pastimes that are controversial in this regard? Apply the preference/principle rationale to them.
5. How do stewards of access and custodians of choice contribute to the very survival of humanity?

EPILOGUE

" ... An 'ecological democracy' requires all of us to tend the soil, and to take care of ourselves as we simultaneously take care of the ground of our being. It requires us to address injustices of all shapes and sizes, and it often requires us to put the needs of others ahead of our own, fortified by the knowledge that caring for the ecology of our world is also caring for ourselves in the long run. "

—The authors

12

Rethinking Recreation and Leisure
in Contemporary Life
An Ecopsychological Perspective

"Only that day dawns to which we are awake. There is more day to dawn.
The sun is but a morning star."

—Henry David Thoreau

In the book *Ecopsychology: Restoring the Earth-Healing the Mind*, psychologist James Hillman asserts that "there is only one core issue for all psychology. Where is the 'me'? Where does the 'me' begin? Where does the 'me' stop? Where does the 'other' begin?... For most of its history, [Hillman continues], psychology located this 'me' within human persons defined by their physical skin and their immediate behavior. The subject was simply 'me in my body and in my relations with other subjects.' The familiar term that covered this entire philosophical system was the 'ego,' and what the ego registered were called 'experiences'" [1]

This conventional Western notion of the self, what Zen philosopher Alan Watts called the "skin-encapsulated ego," [2] is familiar to us all. For the most part, we have been brought up to see ourselves as separate and distinct from one another, as autonomous beings. We view the epidermis as our outermost boundary, as the frontier between us and everything else. It is where we make the cut between I and Thou. This cut results in a way of interpreting the world that is fraught with dichotomies. We categorize phenomena as "this" or "that" and "us" or "them." We divide the Earth up into parcels and label them "my," "your," "our," or "their" property. This leads us, in turn, to a preoccupation with individualism and individual rights, and the peculiar notion that it's possible for one person to prosper in the midst of other people's suffering. The skin-encapsulated ego also provides the grist for social critics like Garrett Hardin, who speaks pejoratively of our apparent incapacity to see beyond our own immediate self-interests, and therefore, of the absolute necessity to coerce us all into socially responsible behavior.[3]

This separation of "me" from "you," and "us" from "them," has always been looked askance upon by the poets, philosophers, and artists among us. Think, for example, of John Donne's "No Man is an Island," John Muir's "everything is hitched to everything else in the universe," and Ansel Adam's "Not Man Apart." But it is only in the age of ecology that science has begun to demonstrate to our increasing satisfaction that separation and autonomy are ill-conceived descriptors of the human condition, that interconnectedness and interdependence are more illustrative of the way things really are. From Aldo Leopold's *A Sand County Almanac* to Rachel Carson's *Silent Spring*, we are reminded of an intricately woven web of life of that we are but a small part, a web, as environmental philosopher Holmes Rolston puts it, that is not simply the ground under our feet, but the very ground of our being.[4] It is no wonder that one of the preeminent zoologists of our time, Gregory Bateson, has characterized the skin-encapsulated ego as a principal epistemological error of Occidental civilization. [5]

What we are left to ponder are the implications of this misdirected psyche, a certain wrongheadedness that makes it possible for us to see ourselves as being detached from, and oftentimes superior to, everything else. As William James portrayed us so long ago, we are afflicted with a certain kind of blindness with regard to the feelings of creatures and people different from ourselves. [6] Consumed by our own constructions of reality, we fail to see the possibility of other constructions, and, therefore, the possibility of changing ourselves. But if ecology teaches us anything, it is that change we must—both our ways of being and behaving. And this brings us back to the question of the self. So we invite you to consider with us the prospects for shedding the skin-encapsulated ego, however well it may have suited us in the past, in favor of something more compatible, something more harmonious with the larger living world. We invite you to join in the refrain of the great 20th century chorus led by Aldo Leopold, when he implored us to change our role from conquerors of the land community to plain members and citizens of it. [7]

The Discovery of Unity in Hidden Likenesses

Jacob Bronowski described science as the discovery of unity in hidden likenesses. He went on to divide the scientific process into three steps: 1) the identification of likenesses in nature that heretofore seemed unlike; 2) the piecing together of these likenesses in a way that forms a new unity; and 3) the testing of this new unity in the light of experience and behavior. [8] Using Bronowski's three steps as a stairway, we now make a case for elevating our sense of self, for climbing up and out of our self-absorption to a new vantage point from which to conceive of ourselves in relation to others. First, we identify what we perceive to be key likenesses in three different strands of social scientific thought. Second, we piece together these likenesses in a way that points toward a different way of conceiving of ourselves. Third, we test the significance of this different sense of self in relation to the work we do.

Bronowski himself provides the starting point. "The self," he says, "is not something fixed in my head. If it exists at all, my self is a process; the unending process by which I turn new experience into knowledge." [9] To Bronowski, the self is not so much a noun as it is a verb. The self is always in the process of becoming. "I am not a fixed character," he proclaims, "for I am constantly enlarged by my own experiences. Any definition of the self must allow for this enlargement." [10]

Bronowski's thinking contrasts sharply with Hardin's, who also believes we suffer from severe myopia when it comes to the self. Despite our education, Hardin insists, we are selfish by nature, and, therefore, there is no hope for the enlargement of the self to which Bronowski aspires. We stress this divergence of opinion here because how you feel about our human potential for change will likely determine your receptivity to the idea that our sense of self can expand with increasing wisdom.

Economist Kenneth Boulding, for example, while conceding the power of Hardin's perspective, makes a case for averting Hardin's "tragedy of the commons" by enlarging our sense of self to include the entire community. "Community," Boulding reasons, "is a phenomenon within human society . . . by which the identity of the individual becomes bound up with identification with the group. . . ." [11] "Identity," he continues, "is a very powerful source of decisional behavior. ... Once people are coerced, or even better, persuaded into making sacrifices, their identity becomes bound up with the community ... for which the sacrifices were made." [12] These sacrifices, Boulding contends, tie us together in powerful ways. What once was merely "my" agenda or "your" agenda now becomes "our" agenda. Boulding sees this "comedy of community," as he calls it, coming about only as a consequence of our growing awareness of the workings of the world. The idea of community, he concludes, is learned like everything else.

Boulding, then, like Bronowski, offers us reason for hope. He believes the boundaries we draw around ourselves are, to a considerable extent, arbitrary, and that we can choose to make the cut farther and farther out as we learn more and more about the world and our place in it. He does not think, as Hardin does, that we are condemned to see ourselves in only one way for the duration of our lives. He does not conceive of the self as imprisoning. Metamorphosis is not only possible, it is desirable.

If we turn from the realm of intellectual growth and development to the realm of moral growth and development, we find similar strands of thought. Lawrence Kohlberg and Carol Gilligan have constructed well-tested theoretical windows through which we can observe the ways boys and girls and men and women approach moral reasoning. [13, 14] They describe rudimentary stages of moral development characterized by a Hardin-like self-centeredness, followed by the emergence of empathetic understanding as people gradually begin to take in and feel part of the larger world. While neither Kohlberg nor Gilligan suggest that most of us advance particularly far along this path, they do suggest that as we enlarge the context within which we make our moral choices, we are more likely to temper our actions out of concern and regard for others. Indeed, in the more advanced stages of moral reasoning, we internalize the rationale for our moral decisions in a way that is reminiscent of what Boulding said about the binding effect of sacrifice. We want to feel responsible for our moral choices. We want to call them our own. Once again, the larger point seems to be that we have the capacity to change our ways of thinking, seeing, and, therefore, relating to the larger living world as a consequence of our enhanced understanding of it.

Finally, there are the ethicists. From Aldo Leopold's land ethic,[15] to Albert Schweitzer's reverence for life, [16] to Max Oelschlaeger's view of humankind as Nature's device for keeping track of itself, [17] there does seem to be a discernible movement, however snail-like, toward a more connected and caring way of thinking about our relationship with the natural world. In *The Rights of Nature: a History of Environmental Ethics*, historian Roderick Nash attributes this awakening to our liberal democratic tradition and our ongoing commitment to widening the circle of ethical consideration. [18]

This possibility for transformation is echoed throughout the environmental ethics literature. Paul Shepard speaks of a "self with a permeable boundary ... constantly drawing on and influencing its surroundings, whose skin and behavior are soft zones contacting the world instead of excluding it..." [19]   Elizabeth Roberts challenges us to replace the skin-encapsulated ego with a wider construct of identity, an "ecological self." [20] Joanna Macy calls for a "greening of the self," [21] an expansion of who we are to include all of Nature so that any behavior leading to its destruction will be experienced as self-destruction. Others have gone so far as to suggest that the Earth itself be understood as one living organism. James Lovelock's "Gaia hypothesis" [22] rings sympathetically in the ears of some our most respected natural scientists, including Harvard's E. O. Wilson and Yale's Stephen Kellert, who offer their own "biophilia hypothesis,"[23] positing humankind's inborn emotional affiliation with all living organisms.

There is, in sum, reason to believe that we humans have the capacity to transcend our current limited conception of ourselves, and that we can rise to new heights. There is also reason to believe, given our increased understanding of the ecology of our lives, that it is more important than ever to attempt this kind of growth and development sooner rather than later. But if it is to happen, it will have to spring forth from our intellectual and moral growth ascending in unison. Our learning will have to inform our moral choices in powerful new ways.

Implications for Parks, Recreation, and Tourism

This brings us to the realm of parks, recreation, and tourism and to Rabel Burdge's infamous "So what?" question. Why does what we do matter? In what ways are we relevant? How does what we do make a difference? It's always a good idea, we think, to keep Burdge's challenge in mind. What would a new conception of the self actually mean for the questions we raise in recreation, parks, and tourism? What would it mean for the studies we conduct, for the conclusions we draw, for the constituencies we serve, and for management practices? How would a softening of the boundary between self and others manifest itself in the work we do? How would it help make things better? While our primary intent is to turn these questions over to you for your thoughtful consideration, we will brood over just one area, popular of late, that we think would be greatly affected. We are referring to the benefits of leisure.

As we have written with Tom Goodale, "The benefits approach to understanding and justifying leisure services has been a positive step for our profession. The benefits of leisure are manifold, and leisure scientists and practitioners are working diligently to document them." [24] But as we have also written, the idea of individual benefits is troublesome, because it is rooted in the conventional Western notion of the self, a skin-encapsulated ego that apparently can enjoy the benefits of leisure irrespective of their cost. [25] Indeed, to speak of individual benefits makes little sense to us, because as Robert Ornstein and David Sobel argue persuasively, "...people don't really exist as individuals at all. All our lives are bound together. Individuals and society develop and thrive together. We're primed to live cooperatively, and to touch and nourish others in many ways." [26] To our way of thinking, the benefits of leisure only take on meaning in their social context, because "our individual bodies share a living social body, and the health of each of us depends on our social connectedness." [27] Our concern with the current benefits-based approach to leisure services, then, stems from the definition of the individual underpinning it—a separate and distinct being, capable of experiencing benefits independent of others.

If we humans are, in fact, connected to something larger than ourselves, then the idea of individual benefits based on a conception of a separate self is ill-founded. Such a conception can only lead to false dichotomies, false conclusions, and false claims of benefits. How can what any one of us does be beneficial if it harms others, extracts significant costs from others, or, perhaps, even harms ourselves? The current benefits-based calculations only add up when we separate things out from one another that are, in the final analysis, inseparable—including, and especially, ourselves.

Unfortunately, most of our modern conceptions of recreation and leisure do not make this social connection explicit. The most common definitions of the terms treat them as matters of personal preference. Our field's approach to these phenomena in recent years has been decidedly psychological. Our unit of analysis has been the person, the autonomous "I." But if the "I" has been the domain of psychology, and the "we" has been the domain of sociology, the "I" and "we" together have been, increasingly, the domain of ecology. And that, as we have tried to demonstrate, changes everything.

A benefit, from an ecological perspective, is the product of a freely chosen, joyful action that preserves the integrity, stability, and beauty of families, communities, and the environment. Recreation, from an ecological perspective, is the joyful action itself. And leisure, from an ecological perspective, is the atmosphere in which such joyful action is both desirable and possible. ... [28] This ecological perspective evolves quite naturally out of understanding ourselves as part of Nature. Indeed, it is a perspective that points toward seeing ourselves inevitably as being one with Nature.

The magnitude of the resulting implication does not escape us. The work to be done is daunting. It is the equivalent of helping a blind person see. We are also well aware that the softening of boundaries to which we have referred, the blurring of well-established lines, the dismantling of conventional definitions and the construction of new ones to take their place, all bring with them their own set of difficulties. We recall USDA Forest Service social scientist, Bev Driver, saying once that he could not study something if he could not draw a box around it, if he could not define it in a way that clearly distinguished it from everything else. Hillman makes a similar point when he asks, "If we can't be sure where the 'me' ends, how can we establish boundaries (or limits) to the field of psychology... ." [29] "If psychology is the study of the subject, and if the limits of the subject cannot be set, then psychology merges willy-nilly with ecology." [30] And so, perhaps, it does.

We are, it seems, at a crossroads. We can continue along the well-traveled path and make the cut close to the skin—this has its pragmatic advantages—a certain precision or exactness of measurement, for example, yet it may well lead to an insular interiority that, in turn, leads to irrelevance in relation to the larger world. Or we can take the path less traveled and make a wider cut, going out as far as we like, to the deep oceans, to the distant stars.

You can, perhaps, by now appreciate our inclination. Sigurd Olson wrote that "the greatest achievement of our flight to the moon is a picture of the earth, a living blue-green planet whirling in the dark endless void of space, and the realization that this is home."[31] While humankind may prefer to live on other planets someday, for now, at least, this is our only home, and we would do well to conserve its treasures and use its resources intelligently. Under the circumstances, Aldo Leopold's corresponding conclusion that the best measure of our success as a species is in the degree to which we extend ethical consideration to other people, other living things, and, ultimately, the Earth in its entirety, makes perfect sense to us. We cannot, for the life of us, find it within ourselves to argue against this point of view. It is too compelling.

Conclusion

Historian Theodore Roszak tells us that the father of psychotherapy, Sigmund Freud, believed a feeling of oneness with the world was infantile. But Freud also acknowledged at least one set of circumstances under which the ego is willing to give up its sense of separateness. "The ego seems to maintain clear and sharp lines of demarcation," Freud said. "There is only one state—admittedly an unusual state, but not one that can be stigmatized as pathological—in which it does not do this. At the height of being in love, the boundary between ego and object threatens to melt away. Against all the evidence of the senses, a [person] who is in love declares that 'I' and 'you' are one, and is prepared to behave as if it were a fact." [32]

Roszak challenges us to enlarge that thought, to let it "reach beyond our social relations to embrace all we have learned of the intricate bond that exists between ourselves and the biosphere that gives us life. Let the 'you' become the Earth and all our fellow creatures upon it. ...," he says. "Somewhere within this emerging vision of biospheric wholeness lies a new, ecologically based conception of the psyche." [33]

We would like to think that park, recreation, and tourism professionals have a significant educational role to play in nurturing this ecologically based conception of the psyche. In this role, the definitions we use matter. How we conceive of ourselves influences how we study ourselves and what we end up saying about ourselves and how we manage park, recreation, and tourism resources for ourselves. Where we make the cut is critical. Throughout this book, we have argued for a wider swath. We have argued for seeing our skin not as a barrier between self and others, but as a porous membrane through which we connect with others. We have argued for conceiving of the self as a verb rather than a noun, as an ongoing process of change highlighted by an ever-expanding sense of connection to everything else. We have argued for seeing people not as separate from Nature, but as being part of Nature. To us, people and environment are one in the same.

Imagine, for a moment, driving along the Tamiami Trail through Florida's Everglades in the twilight hours of a summer's evening. Suddenly, there on the highway in front of you, is a scavenging bird, feasting on the remains of a recently departed colleague. What are you to do? Do you barge ahead in some sort of Darwinian fit, with little regard for anything or anyone other than yourself? Do you brake out of a sense of altruism that denies yourself for the sake of the other? Or do you brake because you feel—in your bones—that doing harm to this creature would be doing harm to yourself? Therein lays the heart of the matter.

If we truly love this Earth, we must declare that "we" and "it" are one, and try our best to behave as if it were a fact. "Only that day dawns to which we are awake," Thoreau cries up from the ground of our being. "There is more day to dawn. The sun is but a morning star." [34] As park, recreation, and tourism professionals, we are fortunate to be able to participate in this great awakening. We believe we can and should contribute to the cultivation of an ecological self, a self that can grow in harmony with our increased understanding of, and appreciation for, the wellspring from which all blessings flow.

Discussion Questions

1. How can the "skin-encapsulated ego" prevent us from expanding our relationships with others?
2. What are some philosophical and economic challenges that impede our capacity to see beyond our own immediate self-interests?
3. Explain how intellectual, moral, and ethical development can help us transcend our current limited conception of ourselves.
4. How might our field's focus on the benefits of leisure unwittingly reinforce the "self-encapsulated ego?"
5. Discuss the role park, recreation, and tourism professionals can play in creating an ethic based on an ever-expanding sense of connection to the larger world.

13

People and Nature

Toward an Ecological Model of Health Promotion

"There is nothing more central to the evolution of human society and culture than the responsibility of each generation for the next."

—Thomas Goodale

In *Last Child in the Woods: Saving Our Children from Nature-Deficit Disorder,* [1] journalist Richard Louv pieces together a jigsaw puzzle's worth of scientific evidence to support his claim that humankind is losing touch with its biological moorings in ways that are detrimental to human health—especially the health of children. The United States is 85% urbanized and people have largely abandoned the country to make their living and homes in the city. Urban living is a manifestation of advancing technology, which makes it possible to work in more sedentary ways, stay inside more, and exercise less. The impact on health is disastrous. Obesity and obesity-related diseases such as high blood pressure, diabetes, congestive heart failure, strokes, and other maladies accompanying an urban sedentary lifestyle are all on the rise. [2]

Louv is especially concerned about the negative effects of urbanization on children. For a variety of reasons, children are also more sedentary, stay inside more, and exercise less. [3, 4] From 2006 to 2007, participation in outdoor activities dropped 11.6% among U.S. children aged 6 to 17 years and the trend continues. [5] Children spend inordinate amounts of time watching television, playing video games, sitting at their computers, and attending movies. [6] Pergams and Zaradic have even coined a new term, *videophilia*, to describe this growing human inclination to be preoccupied with sedentary activities involving electronic media.

The increasing divide between people and nature jeopardizes human physical and mental health in significant ways. [7] Research has shown, for example, that exposure to nature through early life experiences is integral to children's physical, emotional, and cognitive development. [8, 9, 10] Playing outside is good for children. As adults, these same childhood experiences serve as a foundation for environmental advocacy. [11, 12] To the extent that today's children play outdoors less, their personal growth and development are hampered as is the likelihood they will be environmental advocates upon reaching adulthood. Left unchecked, future citizens may end up detached from their fundamental ground of being and lose sight of their dependence on nature for its life-giving sustenance. Such ecological ignorance would then pose an even greater threat to human and environmental health.

Louv's prescription for what ails children is a heavy dose of nature. His remedy is based on the health benefits of active living and the health-restoring properties of natural environments. His thinking is rooted in the work of environmental psychologists who reason that humankind has spent most of its evolutionary history in close contact with the natural world in ways that have nurtured a deep affinity for it. [13, 14] From this perspective, migration to the city has happened in the blink of an evolutionary eye, and people are now out of sorts with their own biology.

The Urban Condition

Thinking of contemporary human beings as products of a long history that began in the African savanna is a theme that has been developed in the environmental psychology literature. [15, 16, 17, 18, 19] Having spent most of the past in close proximity to nature, environmental psychologists suggest humans may be "wired" for a world they no longer inhabit. Closeness to, and fondness for, nature has been cut off by the relatively recent arrival in the city. Detached from their biological moorings, people are now fundamentally out of step with their own nature, resulting in numerous health problems associated with the urban condition.

This separation between people and nature is reflected in many aspects of city life. People reside in built environments that do not lend themselves to physical activity or outdoor recreation. In most cases, transportation corridors are designed for motorized vehicles rather than bicycle or foot traffic. People work downtown and live in the suburbs. Longing for suburbia has led to urban sprawl, resulting in great distances between work and home. People spend large amounts of time and consume huge amounts of non-renewable fossil fuels commuting to and from work over pavement that is simply too far, or too dangerous, to walk or to ride on a bicycle.

Urban lifestyles separate people from nature as well. Home from work or school, individuals 15 years and older spend approximately 2 hrs 30 min each day watching television, with the remainder of leisure time devoted to bits and pieces of activity that can be measured in minutes. [20] Meanwhile, younger children spend as much as 6 hrs a day in front of one screen or another. [21] Robinson and Godbey report that U.S. citizens spend 95% of the time indoors, leaving little time for outdoor activity. [22]

The cumulative effect of city life on urbanites is a form of inertia, a sedentariness that permeates daily living and results in stresses and strains on people's minds and bodies. Obesity among all segments of the population is on the rise in the United States as is stress. [23, 24] Exacerbating the situation is an uneven distribution of wealth and uneven access to leisure opportunities within the cityscape that make some neighborhoods and some residents even more at risk of urban-related sicknesses. [25, 26, 27] According to Godbey, the ultimate remedy for the collective affliction requires a comprehensive redesign of cities based on mixed use zoning and "smart growth" principles that facilitate getting outside, getting active, and getting back to nature. [28] The monumentality of the challenge is staggering, but to give up on it would be to surrender the health of 85% of the citizenry. Consequently, it behooves park, recreation, and tourism professionals now more than ever to articulate what they can contribute to health promotion in the context of contemporary urban life.

The Health Benefits of Outdoor Recreation

A growing body of knowledge demonstrates the significant health benefits derived from outdoor recreation. Studies linking increased physical activity and increased physical fitness with access to local parks and greenways are evident in the literature, [29, 30, 31, 32] as are studies linking well-placed and well-maintained local parks and greenways with healthy communities. [33] Clearly, health promotion power in outdoor recreation is evidenced by the numerous physiological and psychological benefits associated with experiencing outdoor environments. [34, 35]

What the research suggests to date are strong positive correlations between outdoor recreation participation and beneficial health outcomes. People who participate in outdoor recreation are in disproportionately good health, and people in good health participate disproportionately more in outdoor recreation. [36] The biggest health benefits accrue to people who make a habit of outdoor recreation participation, and the best opportunities to experience beneficial health outcomes from outdoor recreation participation are close to home in the form of municipal park and recreation settings. [37]

While the circumstantial evidence documenting the health promotion power of outdoor recreation engagements is persuasive, drawing specific causal inferences about health outcomes from those engagements is problematic. This problem is due, in part, to methodological shortcomings that take participant self-reports at face value, [38] rely on participants' faulty memories of past outdoor recreational involvement, [39] and treat outdoor recreation pursuits as if they were one activity when they are frequently made up of multiple activities. More importantly, the field's heavy reliance on survey research does not lend itself to causal inference. There is a glaring need for experimental research that probes causation, which has the potential to lead to strong causal inference.

Despite these methodological issues, Godbey concluded that ample evidence supports the assertion that recreating in the outdoors contributes to human health in broad and inter-related ways. [40] Sallis, Prochaska, and Taylor reinforced this assertion by claiming that the association between physical activity and being outdoors is so strong that being outdoors is the best predictor of preschool children's physical activity. [41] Yet there are numerous obstacles preventing the population in general and children in particular from enjoying nature. Unequal access to and information about local park and recreation opportunities are major barriers, [42, 43] as is parental concern for children's safety, a decline in unstructured free play time, poorly designed outdoor spaces, and the litigious nature of society. [44] These obstacles must be overcome if adults and children alike are to be reacquainted with their natural heritage.

The importance of removing constraints to outdoor recreation participation cannot be overemphasized. The health benefits of regular unstructured time outdoors for children are multifaceted. They include more creative play, more active imaginations, lower stress levels, increased fitness, stronger immune systems, fewer symptoms of Attention Deficit Disorder and Attention Deficit Hyperactivity Disorder, and increased self-respect, respect for others, and respect for the environment. [45] Outdoor play settings facilitate children's most powerful form of learning—learning by doing—and the outdoors may provide the best context for children to understand the workings of the larger world. [46]

Moreover, exercising the human body is critical to enhancing human health, and outdoor recreation provides what may be the best opportunity for people to move in an enjoyable and sustainable manner. Opportunities for exercise in work or household-related activities are intermittent as are opportunities specifically to improve health (e.g., fitness centers). [47] The best hope for sustaining exercise may be when it is an inherent part of a pleasurable experience. Enhanced health then becomes a byproduct of doing something one finds joy in, something intrinsically motivating, and something that has staying power, [48, 49] which may be the unique contribution of recreation engagements to health promotion.

Nature's Restorative Potential

Researchers have also addressed whether health benefits differ between natural and built environments. [50, 51, 52] Their findings suggest that people not only prefer natural environments to built environments, they also perceive that natural environments offer them greater potential for positive experiences. The tendency to think of and respond to natural environments more positively may be because they allow people to recover from the stresses and strains of daily living. [53, 54] Stress reduction, considered to be a major benefit of parks and open space since Olmsted and Vaux designed New York City's central park in the middle of the 19th century, [55, 56] may be the single most important therapeutic outcome that increasing contact with the natural world offers contemporary urban dwellers. [57]

The health benefits of an active outdoor lifestyle also extend from people to nature. When people get out of their houses and cars and set out on a bicycle or on foot, they reduce the demand for limited non-renewable fossil fuels, thereby reducing air pollution and global warming. To the extent these activities are sustained over time, all will be able to enjoy cleaner air to breathe and cleaner water to drink. The health of the environment itself will likely improve as the collective load is lightened and the carbon footprint is reduced. A healthier environment will then be in better shape to give back health benefits of its own. Parks and greenways, for example, can mitigate air pollution and reduce increased temperatures. [58, 59] However, to realize these benefits, green spaces and accessible pathways must be designed into the cityscape in ways that improve both human health and the health of the underlying ecological system. [60, 61]

The health-restoring properties of natural environments are even more far reaching. S. Kaplan's work on Attention Restoration Theory suggests that interactions with nature can reverse directed attention fatigue, an affliction common to the pressurized modern world. [62] The effort involved in focusing attention on work-related tasks is exhausting, and S. Kaplan theorized that encounters with nature replenish fatigued directed attention capacity. Something appears to be inherently therapeutic about communing with nature.[63] Even children with Attention Deficit Disorder benefit from nature's healing properties. [64, 65] Finally, small doses of nature in the midst of an urban setting yield micro-restorative experiences.[66] In a landmark study of a hospital setting, Ulrich found that patients recovering from surgery who had a window overlooking a natural scene recovered more quickly than patients whose view overlooked a built environment. [67] These, and similar findings, have spawned new efforts to design buildings, towns and cities that weave more greenery into the fabric of urban landscapes. [68, 69]

An Ecological Model of Health Promotion

In sum, like a pianist's glissando, the preventive power of active outdoor living sounds healthy notes emanating from the individual to the larger environment, while the therapeutic power of a healthier environment reverberates back to the individual by sounding healthy notes of its own. The resulting harmony reflects the striking of symbiotic keys. The individual, through a healthier lifestyle, reduces his or her carbon footprint on the larger world, while the larger world reciprocates with cleaner air, cleaner water, and an abundance of health-restoring properties.

This symbiosis demonstrates that health is a dynamic relationship that can best be understood by conceiving it in broad ecological terms. Health, from an ecological perspective, is a measure of the wellness of the individual and the community considered together. The individual cannot be healthy independent of the condition of the larger community, and the larger community cannot be healthy independent of the condition of the individuals constituting it. Healthy individuals require healthy families, healthy families require healthy communities, healthy communities require healthy nations, healthy nations require a healthy planet, and vice versa. Health, at its core, is symbiotic in nature. [70]

This ecological approach to health promotion frames the interconnectedness and interdependence of the natural and physical attributes of the world into a more coherent and systematic way of thinking. It illustrates the harmonious potential that should define humankind's relationship with the larger world. As Figure 1 shows, there is a strong symbiotic relationship between ecosystem health and the health of the functional units that make up ecosystems, including humans. The model also recognizes the role humans play in affecting ecosystems as well as ecosystem effects on humans. The emphasis is on sustaining the health of the planet as a whole as well as its interdependent parts.

When evaluating the relationship between a healthy planet and sustaining healthy people, communities, and nations, the intricacy of this vast web of interrelationships becomes clear. Think of global climate change and its associated health-related reverberations all the way down to the level of individual life forms. At the same time,

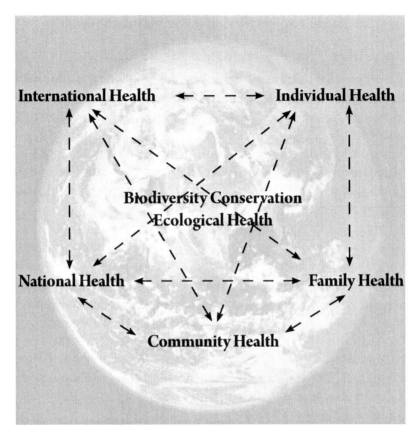

the model reflects how an environmentally friendlier code of human conduct has the potential to reverberate outward resulting in large scale environmental improvements. Individual human beings can deliver health benefits to the planet, while a healthier planet can reciprocate by:

- Filtering toxic substances from the air, water, and soil;
- Protecting against flooding, storm surges, and erosion;
- Breaking down wastes and recycling substances;
- Pollinating crops and wild plant species;
- Creating and maintaining soil fertility;
- Sequestering carbon that mitigates global climate change;
- Helping maintain the water cycle and stabilize local climates;
- Feeding, clothing, and sheltering us; and
- Giving us a host of other goods and services that support life, including human life on Earth. [71]

These ecosystem "services" not only fill fundamental biological needs, they also fill cultural needs for recreational, aesthetic and spiritual well-being. [72]

Further, people depend on the planet for medicines that originate from diverse types of ecosystems. These ecosystems also help understand disease, support the food web upon which people depend, and reduce the risks of contracting infectious diseases. [73, 74] Knowing all this, the planet is rarely placed front and center in thinking about how to conceptualize health in society. Humankind's dependency on a healthy planet is obscured by affluence in the Western industrialized world, while the world's poorest countries have no such economic buffer to shield them from their direct dependence on the health of the planet for their welfare. [75]

Conservation of biodiversity is the centerpiece for sustaining health in all of its manifestations. Threats to biodiversity and the consequences of its losses, including the obvious ecological consequences as well as the impact on aesthetic, ethical, sociological, and economical aspects of our world, reveal the reality of dependence on a healthy planet. The significance of these relationships extends from the local to the global level, affecting the health not only of individual human beings, but of the earth as a whole. Put simply, humans depend on the health of other species and on the "healthy functioning of natural ecosystems" [76] for their own personal health. What an ecological model of health promotion demonstrates is that individual, familial, communal, national, international and global health is highly intertwined and interdependent. Negative perturbations in any of the functional units may have untold negative rippling effects on the earth as a whole, thereby diminishing its ability to deliver ecosystem services of its own. The model also reflects the central role that humans play for better or worse in health promotion. The overarching lesson is that for the earth to deliver its products and non-material benefits to humankind, its health must be looked after as well.

Toward a More Comprehensive Health Promotion Strategy

An ecological model of health promotion implies that the benefits of parks, recreation, and tourism inevitably will be measured by the degree to which they help sustain the health of all life. In this regard, encouraging and facilitating active outdoor living is an affordable proactive strategy for averting many of the chronic diseases plaguing the sedentary urban population. Preventing health problems is simply cheaper than paying for medical treatment after the fact. For this reason alone, parks, recreation, and tourism services should be embraced as part of a comprehensive health promotion strategy. If physical, mental, and emotional well-being can be improved by walking, hiking, biking, climbing, running rivers, skiing, snowboarding, snowshoeing, and a host of other outdoor pursuits, [77, 78] then these activities should be considered integral to a common sense cure for what ails people, a cure made all the more palatable by mounting scientific evidence demonstrating their efficacy and cost effectiveness.

At the same time, getting back to nature can help restore the earth's health. This possibility requires careful consideration of the ways in which people act when recreating in the outdoors. Choosing recreational pastimes that reduce the carbon footprint and help restore nature's ability to deliver ecosystem services is essential to the reciprocity upon which health depends in its broadest sense. Focusing on human health alone runs the risk of ignoring the harm that can be done to the health of the planet by some forms of outdoor recreation. In the long run, this harm could diminish human health as well through a gradual erosion of the quality of outdoor recreation opportunities and environments. [79] People cannot be healthy if the planet on which they live is unhealthy. The planet on which people live cannot be healthy if people persist in unhealthy human behaviors. Health is a harmonious ecological relationship that must be nurtured constantly.

New Research Directions

Appreciating health as a symbiotic relationship rooted in ecological understanding suggests a new orientation to studying the health promotion power of outdoor recreation engagements. On a macro level, interdisciplinary efforts are required to better understand the dynamics of the ecosystemic properties of health. As Godbey recommended, this approach would include research investigating synergistic potentials in community design and zoning, transportation, school policy, park and recreation policy, market-sector outdoor recreation opportunities, climate change, demographic change and other contributors to, or inhibitors of, health promotion. [80] Such an ecological orientation would be based on the realization that the major determinants of health have less to do with the health care system per se than with the environmental and social aspects of health. [81, 82] This is why park, recreation, and tourism settings, especially those located close to home, may be ideally situated to foster health. [83]

Lack of contact with nature is a growing problem with effects only now beginning to be understood. Evidence suggests that the disconnect results in serious negative health consequences. Additional research is needed to better understand nature's health-restoring properties, the barriers to benefiting from those properties (especially for children), and how to break down those barriers. A particularly important sub-context to this line of inquiry is the decreasing amount of children's free play time in the outdoors. The costs and benefits of highly structured play for children need to be better understood as well as the ways in which children benefit from unstructured outdoor play. Laboratories abound for this research, including neighborhood vacant lots, school yards, local parks, and organized camps.

As outdoor recreation trends research has shown, participation patterns are highly skewed and outdoor recreation planners and policymakers must provide opportunities that are more appealing to ethnic minorities and women. [84, 85] Park, recreation, and tourism professionals must better understand the interests of ethnic minorities and women as well as the constraints to their participation, and then set about accommodating those interests and removing those constraints. The impetus for this research is rooted in social justice in the provision of park, recreation, and tourism opportunities as well as in a concern for planning for a preferred future that serves the needs of all citizens. [86]

A rapidly aging population should also be the focus of increased research attention. Current estimates indicate that one in five U.S. citizens is 65 years or older and this percentage will more than double by the middle of the century. [87] People are also living longer and the number of citizens 85 years or older will triple by

2050. Planning environmentally friendly and sustainable outdoor recreation opportunities for a much larger older population with declining physical abilities will require forethought and creativity on the part of outdoor recreation planners and policymakers, landscape architects, and other allied health professionals. Interdisciplinary research that informs this planning process should be a top priority.

Partnerships between parks, recreation, and tourism and allied health agencies must be evaluated as well for their effectiveness in reducing social health care costs. There has been little evaluative research on these partnerships even though parks, recreation, and tourism is now widely recognized as a health promotion profession.[88] Initial efforts by Driver and others to program specifically for health-related benefits is encouraging. [89] Researchers are in the nascent stage of demonstrating the park, recreation, and tourism profession's contributions to human and environmental health. [90] This research should be a primary focus framed by an ecological orientation to health promotion.

The role of tourism in fostering health, especially at the communal, national, and international levels, also warrants heightened attention. The potential health benefits emanating from a maturing tourism industry dedicated to social and environmental responsibility and sustainability need to be better documented to illustrate the industry's contributions to health in its broadest contexts—sustainable economic development, enhanced cross-cultural understanding, friendship, and peace. [91, 92]

Finally, the costs as well as the benefits of outdoor recreation engagements must be factored into the health promotion equation.[93] This focus is necessary to establish a sustainable foundation for enlightened service delivery. At its core, everything depends on the health of the planet. An ecological perspective makes this core clear. It illustrates the critical role of parks, recreation, and tourism in enhancing the quality of life for individuals, families, communities, nations, and the world at large. The park, recreation, and tourism profession, as much as any other profession is well-suited and well-positioned to help create a healthy sustainable future. By this same test, this profession must dedicate itself and its resources to the joyful promotion of health as a fundamental quest.

Conclusion

An ecological model of heath promotion is rooted in a worldview that sees humankind as a part of nature. Western civilization has challenged this view from Descartes to the present day, [94] but advances in ecology reaffirm humankind's physiological, psychological, and spiritual rootedness in the natural world. [95] The ongoing challenge is to embrace this ecological reality and reconnect with nature in ways that contribute to the individual and collective health of all living things. The challenge is particularly crucial to the healthy growth and development of children on whose behalf today's adult population bears the burden of responsibility. As Goodale avowed, "There is nothing more central to the evolution of human society and culture than the responsibility of each generation for the next."[96] With this responsibility in mind, it is time to acknowledge and advocate for the park, recreation, and tourism profession's centrality to the resolution of many health-related problems plaguing sedentary and urbanized ways of life.

Discussion Questions

1. How does the increasing divide between people and nature jeopardize human physical health? Give examples documented in the literature.
2. How can the park, recreation, and tourism profession contribute to solving the "nature-deficit disorder" of modern youth?
3. What role does outdoor recreation play in a healthy lifestyle? Why is this role in doubt in our modern, urbanized way of life?
4. Discuss how an ecological model of health promotion can be linked to park, recreation, and tourism services and facilities.
5. What research topics and approaches are needed to investigate the health promotion power of outdoor recreation engagements?

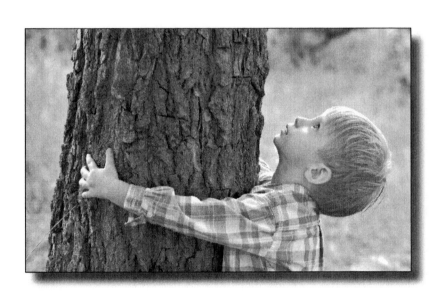

14

Ecological Democracy

Cultivating Healthy Citizens

"In the upside-down world of America today, our culture's dysfunctional message is that healthy people accept the world as it is. We are taught that problems are pervasive and insolvable, and that we are powerless. Also, we hear that only radical nuts or quixotic fuzzy-brains work for social and political change. Yet powerlessness produces despair in people and stagnation in cultures. Throughout history, it has been the strong people who have endeavored to make their communities better. Healthy people act."

—Mary Pipher

This book has rested on one central premise—people are part of nature. As such, human health depends on nature's health. That was the theme of the last chapter. The question now becomes, "If we are to leave the world a better place—a healthier place—than when we arrived in it, how can we conduct our lives in ways that contribute to a more caring and connected relationship with the larger community of life?"

On the face of it, this does not appear to be an insolvable problem. We are individuals embedded in community, and we have it within our power to do whatever it takes to create a meaningful, fulfilling, and sustainable way of life. Surely, we do not need "radical nuts" or "quixotic fuzzy-brains" to carry out social and political change on our behalf. Surely, we have the willpower and the brainpower to effect the necessary change ourselves.

Yet, as discussed throughout these pages, a multitude of factors inhibits active involvement in a participatory democracy. Chief among them are entrenched beliefs, attitudes, and behaviors grounded in a longstanding worldview that sees humankind as separate from and superior to nature, as well as being conquerors and controllers of nature. This worldview is often reinforced by a strong sense of individualism and autonomy that permeates our collective psyche and discourages us from participating in public life. We attend to our own personal needs and expect elected and appointed officials to mind our public needs. Disengagement from public life has made it easier for a variety of special interests to unduly influence public policy, resulting in all kinds of social, political, and environmental problems. If we are to fix things, we have much work to do on our individual and collective psyches, as well as on our sense of responsibility for the world around us.

The purpose of this book, then, is not quite complete. The ground work is done—the spading, the tilling, the fertilization in preparation for the planting—but the seed to be sown has yet to be discussed. The remainder of this chapter is devoted to explaining just what is it that a participatory democracy ought to cultivate in the context of parks, recreation, and tourism.

Three Conceptions of Self

To get at the root of the matter, let us consider three ways we might conceive of ourselves in relation to everything else: the self as part, the self as whole, and the self as part and whole.

Thinking of our individual selves as merely part of something larger means we are likely to see ourselves as having value only to the extent we serve the interests of a larger whole, be it family, business, community, nation, or world. In and of ourselves, we amount to little really. We are as cogs in a large machine. We are but interchangeable parts, and what fulfillment we do experience resides in the fulfillment of the larger whole. This is the psychology of the collective, reinforced by the belief that when the whole does well, so do all of its constituent parts.

Conversely, to think of ourselves as individual wholes means we are likely to interpret self-fulfillment largely in terms of what we alone accomplish. Because we see our individual selves as autonomous and complete, we feel we can experience fulfillment independent of the condition of the rest of the world. This view of the self as a solitary whole leads us to believe that looking out for our own individual self-interests will advance the interests of the collective. We are inclined to look inward for motivation, initiative, and drive. We are also inclined to look inward for reassurance and security, and to rely on our own strengths to overcome life's challenges. This is the psychology of self-reliance.

Ecological understanding offers yet a third view of the self— the self as whole and part. Ecology tells us that while we may be autonomous wholes in a physiological sense, we are tied to a much larger ecological web of life in a social-biological sense. From this perspective, we are both whole and part. This ecological perspective is not just an abstract philosophical viewpoint; it is scientifically informed and supported. It tells us that when we focus on our "autonomous self" only, our behavior tends toward self-aggrandizement rather than self-fulfillment. Our behavior is fueled by a "me-first" psychology.[1] Ecological insight reminds us, however, that it is only when we accept the interconnected nature of our existence as whole and part, and behave accordingly, that we open up the possibility of experiencing self-fulfillment in its larger sense. Self-fulfillment comes only when the integrity of the larger ecological system is also assured. From this perspective, self-fulfillment complements the fulfillment of other actors in the surrounding ecosystem. A political, economic, and social system that considers the ecological realities of life fits well with this view of the self as whole and part. Seeing ourselves this way encourages us to develop a system of social organization and governance that supports the communal good of all life on the planet, while still attending to our own individual needs.

Democracy is often seen as a preferred avenue for seeking self-fulfillment, yet even as we strongly advocate for people's participation in the democratic process, there is little agreement about what it really means to say our country is democratic. What the authors of this book mean by democracy is that people—all people—should truly be the ones ruling themselves and making their own decisions, while respecting and exhibiting tolerance for other voices.

Seeing ourselves as whole and part encourages us to call on the individualistic part of ourselves to work for the public part of ourselves. We may look inward for motivation, initiative, and drive, but our social-biological connectedness to the larger community of life should steer us in a direction that promotes the public welfare. We must strive to understand that our individual fulfillment is intertwined with the fulfillment of the larger world of which we are but a part. The individual self must also be a healthy self in order to fulfill its larger purpose, and a healthy self is intimately intertwined with environmental health. Health is a symbiotic relationship. [2]

The authors have advocated for a worth ethic based on three fundamental tenets: respect as a birthright, freedom to grow, and opportunities for choice. When health is added into the mix, we have the essential ingredients to cultivate rich and rewarding lives. What we do with our lives, of course, is largely up to each of us. We have to contribute our own talent, drive, commitment, perseverance, and all those other qualities that our highly individualistic selves contain. We have to tend to our own lives. But our social conscience should help us pare individualistic, self-aggrandizing tendencies and keep us on a more ecologically sustainable path. In the end, we are obliged to conduct our lives in an ecologically responsible manner, because we understand that our welfare, our children's welfare, and their children's welfare, are inextricably bound up with the welfare of the larger world. We are thus moved to look beyond the benefits of any immediate harvest and consider the harvests of generations to come.

Increasingly, being part of the "whole" is being part of something larger than our local community. We have evolved into an interdependent global economy and an ecologically interdependent planet. Actions of any one country affect all others economically, socially, culturally, and environmentally. Beyond ourselves and our descendents, we are thus required to consider the harvests of humankind in distant parts of the globe as well.

In Consideration of the Ecological Self

The million-dollar question, of course, is can we change our entrenched beliefs, attitudes, and behaviors? We know that we should make changes to tend to the physical, ecological, and social health of the world. We know we should do something, but do we have the individual and collective resolve to take on such a daunting challenge? Can we change the way we conceive of ourselves? Can we expand our sense of self? As discussed in the opening pages of this book, Garrett Hardin did not think so. He reasoned that our selfish, myopic tendencies are largely intractable, and that we must accept ourselves for who we are and manage ourselves accordingly.[3] Kenneth Boulding, on the other hand, reasoned that when we make sacrifices for the sake of the part of us that is connected to the larger living world, the "comedy of community" [4] as he called it, our identities become bound up with that world. In effect, our sense of self grows and we are more inclined to exercise restraint because we recognize ourselves as whole and part, and we understand that our sacrifices serve us and the world we reside in simultaneously.

While Hardin's logic is persuasive, recent criticisms of it give new strength to Boulding's perspective. Scholars have begun to illustrate that privatized ideas of nature—often supported by Hardin's arguments—characterize human behavior as being determined by individual, material self-interest. Such ideas:

> . . . privilege an abstract version of conservation, in which nature is measured by desocialized science and given value through the logic of supply and demand. It then seeks policies that will maximize environmental-market efficiency and thus yield the greatest conservation gain at the least cost for abstract 'society.' Actual society, with its place-specific complexities and unruly actors, is set aside. The historically contingent, unequal distribution of economic power and property rights in the market world is taken for granted. [5]

In *Earth Democracy*, [6] scholar/activist Vandana Shiva provides numerous examples of communities that have averted the "tragedy of the commons" through shared understanding and commitment to accessing and protecting the integrity of commonly held resources, whether these resources are material goods or community knowledge. As Shiva puts it:

> Greed, domination, [and] exclusion, are not "essential" human qualities. Functioning commons demonstrate that people can govern themselves, that democratic self-organization and self-governance work, and that people can cooperate, share, and jointly make democratic decisions for the common good. [7]

Shiva reasons that enclosing or privatizing the commons largely serves the interests of the wealthy and powerful at the expense of the people. She grounds her thinking in justice, sustainability, and peace, and provides a positive, hopeful alternative to Hardin's pejorative take on human behavior.

Justice, Virtue, and the Common Good

Ultimately, our book calls for a philosophical foundation for the park, recreation, and tourism profession grounded in a common concern for social and environmental justice. [8]

Michael Sandel, a political philosopher and noted scholar on public morality, describes three differing approaches to justice: 1) a commitment to the greatest good for the greatest number, 2) a commitment to freedom of choice in the open market, and 3) a commitment to cultivating virtue and reasoning about the common good. [9]

Following Sandel's lead, the park, recreation, and tourism profession should favor the third approach to justice and his three "action items" that may lead to a new politics of the common good. The first charge is to cultivate a concern for the whole in the citizenry, a concern for the common good. Park, recreation, and tourism programs and facilities should counteract a purely privatized version of the good life and focus people on civic engagement. Park, recreation, and tourism areas and facilities should be places where people of different ethnic, cultural, and religious backgrounds come together to foster greater tolerance and understanding, and to work for the common good. These areas and facilities should serve as exemplars for citizenship development, sacrifice, and service.

Sandel's second charge is to acknowledge and counteract the moral limits of markets. Market-oriented reasoning and norms should not be allowed to overshadow the norms of social institutions like the family, public schools, health services, and public recreation spaces. The park, recreation, and tourism profession has been engulfed in this struggle with market-oriented norms related to fees and charges for decades, and this book's authors agree with Sandel that it is high time to have a public debate on the moral limits of markets. [10]

Sandel's third charge concerns inequality, solidarity, and civic virtue. The increasing disparity between the rich and poor in America is threatening citizen solidarity and civic virtue. As the affluent increasingly abandon the public schools for private schools, abandon public park, recreation, and tourism facilities for private clubs, and abandon city neighborhoods for gated communities, they are less willing to pay taxes to maintain the infrastructure that supports these social institutions. This economic and social segregation into private facilities for the affluent eliminates opportunities for rich and poor to interact, and threatens the solidarity that participation in community institutions nurtures. Park, recreation, and tourism professionals should help reverse this trend by contributing to an infrastructure for civic renewal. We should provide high quality recreation spaces and programs where both rich and poor parents want to send their children—parks, community centers, libraries, and museums—and that "draw people out of their gated communities and into the common spaces of a shared democratic citizenship." [11]

Cultivating Healthy Citizens

The park, recreation, and tourism profession exists to serve the democratic process and should be largely in agreement with Sandel's third conception of justice—cultivating virtue and reasoning about the common good. Our challenge is to prepare, encourage, and support the citizenry to become more actively engaged in creating, enjoying, and accounting for their existence. We are obliged to tend to the citizenry, and focus our efforts on cultivating healthy, independent functioning, and socially responsible citizens. We are like farmers dedicated to growing self-reflecting, self-regulating people through the work we do. More importantly, we aspire to be like local organic farmers by cultivating socially responsible citizens in our towns and communities while avoiding negative impacts on the surrounding countryside that sustains us.

Talking about cultivating people the way a farmer might talk about cultivating potatoes takes some getting used to, but the parallels are striking. We, too, are toilers in the field, committed to creating the best possible conditions for turning out the best possible people. Our duty is to weed out social and environmental injustices that inhibit healthy, sustainable growth and development. Our duty is to look out for the welfare of individual human beings in the same way we look out for the welfare of endangered plants and animals. We understand that people are part of nature, too, and we are duty bound to liberate people from exploitation and domination in the same way we are duty bound to liberate nature from exploitation and domination. As social ecologist Murray Bookchin reminds us:

> Over the centuries... social conflicts have fostered the development of hierarchies and classes based on domination and exploitation in which the great majority of human beings have been as ruthlessly exploited as the natural world itself. Social ecology carefully focuses on this social history and reveals that the very idea of dominating nature stems from the domination of human by human. This hierarchical mentality and system has been extended out from the social domination of people— particularly young women, people of color, and yes, males generally as workers and subjects—into the realm of non-human nature. Thus... social ecologists understand that until we undertake the project of liberating human beings from domination and hierarchy... our chances of saving the wild areas of the planet and wildlife are remote at best. [12]

Good Growth

Not too long before he died, Edward Abbey declared that "growth for the sake of growth is the ideology of the cancer cell." Abbey's sardonic humor reminds us that the kind of growth we nurture in our fellow human beings matters. There are good and bad forms of growth. As previously noted, there is a problem with growing consumption of physical things in a world of limited non-renewable natural resources. The accumulation of material wealth is not a particularly good measure of how we are faring in life. There are simply not enough physical things to go around. The endless accumulation of wealth, which is a defining paradigm in the developed world, is problematic well beyond the material limitations of the planet. It is socially, psychologically, and environmentally unfulfilling. It is also unsustainable.[13] Loading up our lives with material possessions is just not very satisfying. Consequently, championing material wealth as the best measure of the good life, and defining the accumulation of physical possessions as the best expression of the American Dream, leads our fellow citizens down a path of increasing frustration and disappointment. Indeed, as Philip Slater observed many years ago, sacrificing our lives for the accumulation of dead things is just not a very meaningful way to spend our limited time on this earth. [14]

One of the park, recreation, and tourism profession's most important responsibilities is to educate the citizenry about this distinction between good and bad kinds of growth. There are implications from a "local to global" perspective. From an ecological perspective, sustainable development requires us to consider the wise use of resources, the alleviation of poverty, and the improvement of lives, and to cooperate in addressing societal ills through reversing the loss of environmental resources. [15] As part of a global social and ecological network, we are linked to a larger world, and therefore more than ever, the impact of our actions today, is felt on distant shores. As such,

> We are caught in the paradox that we cannot save the world without saving particular places. But neither can we save our places without national and global policies that limit predatory capital and that allow people to build resilient economies, to conserve cultural and biological diversity, and to preserve ecological integrities. Without waiting for national governments to act, there is a lot that can be done to equip people to find their place and dig in. [16]

Given the multitude of opportunities to address challenges in society within the context of parks, recreation, and tourism—from work in natural resources conservation to working with youth at risk, to utilizing tourism to enhance community development in impoverished areas of the world—we must encourage our constituents to enrich their lives through intellectual, spiritual, and emotional experiences that are, unlike physical possessions, inexhaustible. They can be "consumed" ad infinitum without detracting from the physical world's sum total of limited nonrenewable natural resources. This kind of human growth—an expanding network of mutually rewarding friendships characterized by intellectual, spiritual, and emotional richness—offers us limitless possibilities for meaningful, rewarding, and sustainable life experiences. [17] What better way to think about human growth and development than a lifetime devoted to growing into larger and larger patterns of ecologically sound interrelationships and interdependencies that are meaningful, enjoyable, and sustainable over time?

Experiencing one another's uniqueness, celebrating one another's diversity, and coming together in ways that honor and respect one another's contributions to the welfare of the larger community of life, are admirable goals for us all. To live our lives in increasing harmony with the larger living world, soaring higher and higher in wider and wider arcs of understanding and cooperation that benefit us all—therein is the best expression of the leisure ideal.

Leisure's Promise

What makes leisure so inviting as a field of study is its potential for serving human growth and development. Leisure should not be viewed simply as "free time" or "diversionary activities." Leisure is when we are most free to choose our actions and give them form and meaning. It is when we are most in control of our lives and when we are most answerable for the actions we take. It is when we are freest to make our greatest individual differences. The way we express ourselves in leisure says much about who we are as human beings.

The problems encountered in leisure studies are the same problems encountered across all academic disciplines. The difference is context. Matters philosophical, social, political, and environmental are played out in park, recreation, and tourism settings just as they are in all other dimensions of our lives. So it is that Garrett Hardin's "Tragedy of the Commons," [18] a line of thought rooted in a concern about an overcrowded planet, can be applied to an overcrowded park. So it is that Lawrence Kohlberg and Carol Gilligan's thinking about moral development, [19, 20] generated to better explain the moral choices we make in the day-to-day living of our lives, can be applied to explaining our recreational conduct as well. The list goes on and on, but what makes leisure studies so compelling is the centrality of freedom and choice in the mix. Not coincidentally, these are also the central elements of a functioning participatory democracy. Our leisure behavior is most telling and most reflective of who we are as self-reflecting and self-regulating beings and of who we are collectively in our forms of democratic governance.

How we employ our leisure is a vital part of what it means to live in a participatory democracy. The onus is on each one of us to design our life, carry it out, and accept responsibility for it. Today, while many of us enjoy the various freedoms of democratic organization, there are people on the planet who are less free to determine their own destinies and less able to make their own dreams come true. [21] "What we gain by living in a participatory democracy is both the opportunity and the obligation to educate ourselves and then to take an active role in our nation's growth and development." [22] A democratic system of governance that explicitly acknowledges and integrates the ecological interconnectedness of our world demands constant tending and participation from all of its citizens. An "ecological democracy" requires all of us to tend the soil and to take care of ourselves as we simultaneously take care of the ground of our being. It requires us to address injustices of all shapes and sizes, and it often requires us to put the needs of others ahead of our own, fortified by the knowledge that caring for the ecology of our world is also caring for ourselves in the long run. It is the part of us in service of the whole of us that makes our individual lives worth living. [23] And it is the park, recreation, and tourism profession's responsibility to steward this process of human growth and development while also serving as the custodian of the ecological whole within which this grand unfolding occurs.

Discussion Questions

1. The authors claim that Americans largely see themselves as separate from, and superior to, nature, and as governed by individualism and self-interest. Do you agree? Why or why not?
2. Do you think park, recreation, and tourism professionals can play a significant role in cultivating socially and environmentally responsible citizens? If "yes," how? If "no," why not?
3. Contrast Hardin's pessimistic view of the fate of the "commons" with Shiva's more optimistic view. What are the implications of these differing views for the way in which we look after park, recreation, and tourism resources?
4. How can the park, recreation, and tourism profession educate citizens about the distinction between good and bad kinds of growth?
5. Why is our leisure behavior a telling indication of who we are as human beings?

About the Authors

Kelly Bricker is associate professor in the Department of Parks, Recreation, and Tourism at the University of Utah. She also works part-time as a senior recreation research scientist with HDR/DTA, an environmental planning firm in Sacramento, California. Kelly holds a bachelor's degree in recreation administration and a master's degree in recreation, parks, and tourism administration from Western Illinois University. She completed her Ph.D. research at The Pennsylvania State University, where she focused on sustainable tourism and natural resource management. She has special research and teaching interests in ecotourism, sense of place, natural resource management, and the environmental and social impacts of tourism. Kelly has conducted research on heritage tourism, social impacts of tourism, and natural resource-related tourism environments. She has presented papers on issues in ecotourism, sense of place, natural resource management, and incentive travel programs, and she has published articles on sense of place, ecotourism certification and policy, and health and sustainable tourism relative to communities. With her husband, Nathan, Kelly developed Rivers Fiji, an ecotourism company, and she serves as Chair of The International Ecotourism Society.

Daniel Dustin is professor and chair of the Department of Parks, Recreation, and Tourism at the University of Utah. A past president of the Academy of Leisure Sciences and the Society of Park and Recreation Educators, he holds a bachelor's degree in geography and a master's degree in resource planning and conservation from the University of Michigan and a Ph.D. in education with an emphasis in recreation and park administration from the University of Minnesota. In 1993 he received the National Recreation and Park Association's Literary Award, and in 1994 he was named an honorary lifetime member in the California Park Rangers Association for his contributions to the literature of outdoor recreation planning and policy. Among his recent works as an author and editor are *Speaking Up and Speaking Out: Working for Social and Environmental Justice through Parks, Recreation, and Leisure*; *Service Living: Building Community through Public Parks and Recreation*; *The Wilderness Within: Reflections on Leisure and Life*; *Making a Difference in Academic Life: a Handbook for Park, Recreation, and Tourism Educators and Graduate Students*; and *Nature and the Human Spirit: Toward an Expanded Land Management Ethic.*

Leo McAvoy recently retired from the University of Minnesota, where he enjoys emeritus status. A member of the Academy of Leisure Sciences, he holds a bachelor's degree in psychology from Loras College, a master's degree in recreation administration from San Francisco State University, and a Ph.D. in education with an emphasis in recreation, park, and leisure studies from the University of Minnesota. His research interests are focused on effective wilderness education, inclusive adventure programs, leisure and land management issues, and American Indians. Among his many honors, Leo received the University of Illinois's Allen Sapora Research Award, Indiana University's Reynold Carlson Outdoor Education Achievement Award, the American Association for Leisure and Recreation's Julian Smith Award, and the Minnesota Recreation and Park Association's G. B. Fitzgerald Award. In 2004, Leo's name was added to the University of Minnesota, Minneapolis campus "Scholars Walk," a prominent and permanent memorial to honor his receiving the National Recreation and Park Association's Theodore and Franklin Roosevelt Award for Excellence in Park and Recreation Research.

Jeff Rose is a doctoral candidate in the Department of Parks, Recreation, and Tourism at the University of Utah. He holds a bachelor's degree in mathematics from the University of North Carolina, Chapel Hill, and a master's degree in geography from San Diego State University. Jeff's research is focused on the role of neoliberalism and human-environment relationships in the specific context of a community inhabiting public spaces. He has worked for the past ten years as an outdoor educator. Jeff lives with his partner, dogs, and chickens in Salt Lake City.

John Schultz is the former head of the Division of Recreation, Park, and Leisure Studies at the University of Minnesota. He holds a bachelor's degree in physical education from Valparaiso University, a master's degree in recreation administration from the University of Illinois, and a Ph.D. in education with an emphasis in recreation and park administration from the University of Minnesota. Both Leo McAvoy and Dan Dustin had the privilege of doing their graduate work under John's watchful eye. He is now retired and enjoys living on a farm in southern Minnesota with his wife, Kelly. Among his many honors, John received the Society of Park and Recreation Educators Distinguished Colleague Award and the Minnesota Recreation and Park Association's Distinguished Service Award.

Keri Schwab is a doctoral candidate in the Department of Parks, Recreation, and Tourism at the University of Utah. She holds a bachelor's degree in media arts and design from James Madison University and a master's degree in recreation, parks, and tourism with an emphasis in experiential education from the University of Utah. Her research interests include family leisure, mothers' leisure, and youth development, and her academic publications and presentations have focused on family physical activity, health promotion, educational scaffolding, online learning, and an ecological view of health. Keri's professional background includes working with youth in an after-school program, service coordination for families having children with disabilities, grant writing for a social service agency, and a newspaper reporter.

Notes

Introduction

1. Bernard, N. "The Interpretive Profession—Goals and Philosophies; Excerpts from an Address." *The Interpreter*, Vol. IX, No. 1, Spring 1977, pp. 16-18.
2. Geba, B. "The Roots of Recreation." *California Parks & Recreation*, Vol. 34, No. 3, August/September 1978, p. 6.
3. Schumacher, E. *Small Is Beautiful: Economics as if People Mattered.* New York, NY: Harper & Row Publishers, 1973.
4. Bronowski, J. *Science and Human Values.* New York, NY: Harper Colophon Books, 1975.
5. Leopold, A. *A Sand County Almanac.* New York, NY: Oxford University Press, 1949.
6. Laszlo, E. *The Systems View of The World.* New York, NY: George Braziller, 1972.

Chapter 1 (The Problem)

1. Tilden, F. *The National Parks: What They Mean to You and Me.* New York, NY: Alfred A. Knopf, 1963.
2. Lerner, M. *America as a Civilization.* New York, NY: Simon and Schuster, 1957.
3. Ibid, p. 23.
4. Ibid, p. 25.
5. Tocqueville, A. *Democracy in America. Volume II.* New York, NY: Vintage Books, 1945.
6. Ibid, p. 102.
7. Smith, A. *An Inquiry into the Nature and Causes of the Wealth of Nations.* New York, NY: P. F. Collier & Son, 1909.
8. Tocqueville, p. 107.
9. Ibid, p. 267.
10. Everhart, W. *The National Park Service.* New York, NY: Praeger Publishers, Inc., 1972.
11. Ibid, p 92.

12. Dustin, D., More, T., & McAvoy, L. "The Faithful Execution of Our Public Trust: Fully Funding the National Parks through Taxes." *Journal of Park and Recreation Administration*, Vol. 18, No. 4, Winter 2000, pp. 93-102.
13. Dustin, D., McAvoy, L., & Rankin, J. "Land Ethics in a Culturally Diverse Society." *Trends*, Vol. 28, No. 3, 1991, pp. 25-27.
14. Dulles, F. *A History of Recreation: America Learns to Play.* 2nd Edition. Englewood Cliffs, NJ: Prentice-Hall, Inc., 1965.
15. Sax, J. *Mountains without Handrails.* Ann Arbor, MI.: The University of Michigan Press, 1980.
16. Tocqueville, p. 145.
17. Sax, p. 2.
18. Dulles, p. 397.
19. Lerner, p. 73.
20. Ibid, p. 72.
21. Tocqueville, p. l44.
22. Slater, P. *The Pursuit of Loneliness.* Boston, MA: Beacon Press, 1970.
23. Veblen, T. *The Theory of the Leisure Class; an Economic Study of Institutions.* New York, NY: The Modern Library, 1934.
24. Meyersohn, R. "Abundance Reconsidered." In H. Gans, et al. (Eds.) *On the Making of Americans: Essays in Honor of David Riesman.* University of Pennsylvania Press, 1979, pp. 87-104.
25. Scott, D. "What Would Thorstein Veblen Say? The Nagging Problem of Conspicuous Consumption." In K. Paisley and D. Dustin (Eds.) *Speaking Up and Speaking Out: Working for Social and Environmental Justice through Parks, Recreation, and Leisure.* Champaign, IL: Sagamore Publishing, LLC, 2011, pp. 95-104.
26. Schumacher, E. *Small is Beautiful: Economics as if People Mattered.* New York, NY: Harper Colophon Books, 1973.
27. Sax, p. 76.
28. Hardin, G. "The Tragedy of the Commons." *Science*, 162, December 13, 1968, pp. 1243-1248.
29. See Dustin, D., & McAvoy, L. "'Harding' National Parks." *Environmental Ethics*, Vol. II, No. 1, Spring 1980, pp. 39-44.
30. Hardin, p. 1247.
31. Ibid, p. 1244.

32. See Dustin, D., & McAvoy, L. "The Decline and Fall of Quality Recreation Opportunities and Environments?" *Environmental Ethics*, Vol. IV, No. 1, Spring 1982, pp. 49-57.

Chapter 2 (The Response)

1. Sagoff, M. "Do We Need a Land Use Ethic?" *Environmental Ethics*, Vol. 3, No. 4, Winter 1981, pp. 293-308.
2. Hardin, G. "The Tragedy of the Commons." *Science*, 162, December 13, 1968, pp. 1243-1248.
3. Sagoff, M. "The Philosopher as Teacher: on Teaching Environmental Ethics." *Metaphilosophy*, Vol. 11, Nos. 3 & 4, July/October 1980, pp. 307-325.
4. Sagoff, "Do We Need a Land Use Ethic?" pp. 294-295.
5. Ibid, p. 295.
6. McMahon, J. "Garrett Hardin and the Search for Ecological Morality." *The Living Wilderness*, Spring 1973, pp. 23-29.
7. Tilden, F. *Interpreting Our Heritage*. Chapel Hill, NC: The University of North Carolina Press, 1957.
8. See Dustin, D., & McAvoy, L. "The Decline and Fall of Quality Recreation Opportunities and Environments?" *Environmental Ethics*, Vol. IV, No. 1, Spring 1982, pp. 49-57.
9. Dubos, R. *Man Adapting*. New Haven, CT: Yale University Press, 1965.
10. McHarg, I. *Design with Nature*. Garden City, NJ: Natural History Press, 1969.
11. Dubos, p. 278.
12. Ibid, p. 279.
13. Ibid.
14. Ibid.
15. McAvoy, L. "Management techniques preferred by users and landowners along a state river." In D. Lime (Ed.) *Forest and River Recreation: Research Update*. (Miscellaneous Publication 18-1982). St. Paul, MN: University of Minnesota, 1982, pp. 20-25.
16. Heberlein, T., & Vaske, J. "Crowding and Visitor Conflict on the Bois Brule River." *Technical Report WIS WRC 7704*, Water Resource Center, University of Wisconsin, Madison, 1977.

17. Shelby, B., & Nielsen, J. "Use Levels and User Satisfaction in the Grand Canyon." Paper presented to the annual meeting of the Rural Sociological Society, San Francisco, 1975.
18. Vaske, J. Donnelly, M., & Heberlein, T. "Perceptions of Crowding and Resource Quality by Early and More Recent Visitors." *Leisure Sciences*, Vol. 3, No. 4, 1930, pp. 367-381.
19. Greenleaf, R., Echelberger, H., & Wiley, M. "The Relationship of Expectations, Trail Use Levels, and Backpacker Satisfactions." Paper presented at the National Recreation and Park Association Congress in Phoenix, Arizona, October, 1980.
20. Vaske, et al., p. 377.
21. Ibid, pp. 377-379.
22. Clark, R., Hendee, J., & Campbell, F. "Values, Behavior, and Conflict in Modern Camping Culture." *Journal of Leisure Research*, Vol. 3, No. 3, 1971, pp. 143-159.
23. Driver, B., & Tocher, R. "Toward a Behavioral Interpretation of Recreational Engagements, With Implications for Planning." In B. Driver (Ed.) *Elements of Outdoor Recreation Planning.* Ann Arbor, MI: University Microfilms, 1970, pp. 9-31.
24. Clark, et al., p. 145.
25. See Abbey, E. *The Journey Home.* New York, NY: E.P. Dutton, 1977.
26. See Stone, C. *Should Trees Have Standing?* Los Altos, CA: William Kaufmann, Inc., 1974.
27. Fox, K., & McAvoy, L. "Environmental Ethics: Strengths and Dualisms of Six Dominant Themes." In G. Fain (Ed.) *Leisure and Ethics.* Reston, VA: American Alliance for Health, Physical Education, Recreation and Dance, 1991.
28. White, L., Jr. "The Historical Roots of Our Ecologic Crisis." *Science*, Vol. 155, No. 3767, March 10, 1967, pp. 1203-1207.

Chapter 3 (The Dilemma)

1. Hardin, G., & Baden, J. (Eds.) *Managing the Commons.* San Francisco, CA.: W. H. Freeman and Company, 1977.
2. Hardin, G. "The Tragedy of the Commons." *Science*, 162, December 13, 1968, pp. 1243-1248.
3. Slater, P. *The Pursuit of Loneliness.* Boston, MA: Beacon Press, 1970.

4. Ibid, p. 5.
5. Glazer, N. "Individualism and Equality in the United States." In Gans, H., et al. (Eds.) *On The Making Of Americans: Essays in Honor of David Riesman.* University of Pennsylvania, 1979, pp. 127-142.
6. Ibid, p. 132.
7. Dustin, D. "Leisure: a Futurist's Perspective." *California Parks & Recreation*, Vol. 35, No. 3, August/September 1979, pp. 10-11.
8. Sax, J. *Mountains without Handrails.* Ann Arbor, MI.: The University of Michigan Press, 1980.
9. Ibid, p. 52.
10. Dustin, D., & McAvoy, L. "Interpretation as a Management Tool: a Dissenting Opinion." *The Interpreter*, Vol. XVI, No. 1, Spring 1985, pp. 18-20.
11. McAvoy, L., & Dustin, D. "Indirect Versus Direct Regulation of Recreation Behavior." *Journal of Park and Recreation Administration*, Vol. 1, No. 3, Fall 1983, pp. 13-17.
12. Hendee, J. "No, to Attitudes to Evaluate Environmental Education." *The Journal of Environmental Education*, Vol. 3, No. 3, Spring 1972, pp. 64.
13. Hardin, G. "Living on a Lifeboat." *BioScience*, 24:10, October 1974, pp. 561-568.
14. See Bem, D. *Beliefs, attitudes, and human affairs.* Belmont, CA: Brooks/Cole Publishing Co., 1970.
15. Boulding, K. "Commons and Community: The Idea of a Public." In G. Hardin & J. Baden (Eds.) *Managing the Commons.* San Francisco, CA: W. H. Freeman and Company, 1977, pp. 280-294.
16. Ibid, p 286.
17. Tocqueville, A. *Democracy in America.* Volume II. New York, NY: Vintage Books, 1945.
18. Ibid, p. 129.
19. Leopold, A. *A Sand County Almanac.* New York, NY: Oxford University Press, 1949.
20. Boulding, p. 236.
21. Boulding, K. *The Economy of Love and Fear: A Preface to Grants Economics.* Belmont, CA: Wadsworth, 1973.

22. Olson, S. *Reflections from The North Country.* New York, NY: Alfred A. Knopf, 1977.

Chapter 4 (A Worth Ethic for Parks, Recreation, and Tourism)

1. Adapted from Dustin, D., & Schultz, J. "The Worth Ethic as Our Credo: Yea or Nay?" *Parks & Recreation*, Vol. 16, No. 9, September 1981, pp. 61-63.
2. Fabun, D. *The Dynamics of Change.* Englewood Cliffs, NJ: Prentice-Hall, Inc., 1967.
3. Schumacher, E. *Small is Beautiful: Economics as if People Mattered.* New York, NY: Harper & Row Publishers, 1973.
4. Ibid, p. 100.
5. Fabun, Chapter V, p. 21.

Chapter 5 (Respect as a Birthright)

1. Mumford, L. **The Conduct of Life.** New York, NY: Harcourt, Brace and Company, 1951.
2. Toffler, A. *The Third Wave.* New York, NY: Bantam Books, 1981.
3. Drengson, A. "Shifting Paradigms: from the Technocratic to the Person-Planetary." *Environmental Ethics*, Vol. 2, No. 3, Fall 1980, pp. 221-240.
4. Mumford, p. 14.
5. Ibid, p. 11.
6. Ibid, p. 21.
7. Sullivan, H. *The Interpersonal Theory of Psychiatry.* New York, NY: J. W. Norton & Company, 1953.
8. Fabun, D. *The Dynamics of Change.* Englewood Cliffs, NJ: Prentice-Hall, Inc., 1967.
9. Whitehead, A. *Modes of Thought.* New York, NY: The Macmillan Company, 1938.
10. Sullivan, pp. 308-309.
11. Schweitzer, A. *The Teaching of Reverence for Life.* New York, NY: Holt, Rinehart and Winston, 1965.
12. Schweitzer, A. *The Philosophy of Civilization.* New York, NY: The Macmillan Company, 1957.

13. Schweitzer, The Teaching of. . ., p. 26.
14. Boulding, K. *Beasts, Ballads, and Bouldingisms.* New Brunswick (U.S.A.): Transaction Books, 1980.
15. Schweitzer, *The Teaching of. . .*, p. 26.
16. Ibid, p. 9.
17. Katz, E. "Utilitarianism and Preservation." *Environmental Ethics*, Vol. 1, No. 4, Winter 1979, pp. 357-364.
18. Sagoff, M. "Do We Need a Land Use Ethic?" *Environmental Ethics*, Vol. 3, No. 4, Winter 1981, pp. 293-308.
19. Stone, C. *Should Trees Have Standing?* Los Altos, CA: William Kaufmann, Inc., 1974.
20. Goodpaster, K. "On Stopping at Everything: A Reply to W. M. Hunt." *Environmental Ethics*, Vol. 2, No. 3, Fall 1980, pp. 281-284.
21. Schumacher, E. *Small Is Beautiful: Economics As If People Mattered.* New York, NY: Harper Colophon Books, 1973.
22. Stone, p. 48.
23. Leopold, A. *A Sand County Almanac.* New York, NY: Oxford University Press, 1949.

Chapter 6 (Freedom to Grow)

1. See Stone, C. *Should Trees Have Standing?* Los Altos, CA: William Kaufmann, Inc., 1974.
2. Brightbill, C. *The Challenge of Leisure.* Englewood Cliffs, NJ: Prentice-Hall, Inc., 1960.
3. Ibid, p. l06.
4. Ibid.
5. Leopold, A. *A Sand County Almanac.* New York, NY: Oxford University Press, 1949.
6. Boulding, K. *Beasts, Ballads, and Bouldingisms.* New Brunswick (U.S.A): Transaction Books, 1980.
7. Brightbill, p. 108.
8. Boulding, p. 57.
9. See Dustin, D., McAvoy, L., & Schultz, J. "Recreation Rightly Understood." In T. Goodale & P. Witt (Eds.) *Recreation and Leisure: Issues in an Era of Change.* 3rd edition. State College, PA: Venture Publishing, Inc. 1991, pp. 97-106.

10. Brightbill, p. 107.
11. Hardin, G. "The Tragedy of the Commons." *Science*, 162, December 13, 1968, pp. 1243-1248.
12. Brightbill, p. 107.
13. Ibid, p. 109.
14. Schumacher, E. *Small is Beautiful: Economics as if People Mattered.* New York, NY: Harper Colophon Books, 1973.
15. Glazer, N. "Individualism and Equality in the United States." In Gans, H., et al. (Eds.) *On the Making of Americans: Essays in honor of David Riesman.* University of Pennsylvania, 1979, pp. 127-142.
16. Dustin, D. "Recreational Ethics in a World of Limits." *Parks & Recreation*, Vol. 19, No. 3, March 1984, pp. 48-51, 70.
17. Slater, P. *The Pursuit of Loneliness.* Boston, MA: Beacon Press, 1970.
18. Ibid, pp. 103-109.
19. See Fisher, I. *The Nature of Capital and Income.* New York, NY: Augustus M. Kelley, Publisher, 1965.
20. Dustin, D. "Leisure's Role in Expanding Psychic Income." *Leisure Commentary and Practice*, Vol. III, No. 4, August 1984.
21. Olson, S. *Reflections from the North Country.* New York, NY: Alfred A. Knopf, 1977.
22. Iso-Ahola, S. *The Social Psychology of Leisure and Recreation.* Dubuque, IA: W. C. Brown Co., 1980.
23. Lefcourt, H. "The Function of the Illusions of Control and Freedom." *American Psychologist, 28,* 1973, pp. 417-425.
24. Iso-Ahola, p. 191.
25. Schulz, R. "Effects of Control and Predictability on the Physical and Psychological Well-Being of the Institutionalized Aged." *Journal of Personality and Social Psychology, 33,* 1976, pp. 563-573.
26. Martin, A. "A Historical Perspective." In Martin, P. A. (Ed.) *Leisure and Mental Health: A Psychiatric Viewpoint.* Washington, DC: American Psychiatric Association, 1967, pp. 115-126.
27. Gussen, J. "The Psychodynamics of Leisure." In Martin, P. A. (Ed.) *Leisure and Mental. . .*, pp. 51-70.

28. Glazer, p. 12-29.
29. Slater, p. 109.
30. McAvoy, L., & Dustin, D. "Indirect Versus Direct Regulation of Recreation Behavior." *Journal of Park and Recreation Administration*, Vol. 1, No. 3, Fall 1983, pp. 13-17.
31. Dustin, D., & McAvoy, L. "The Limitation of the Traffic Light." *Journal of Park and Recreation Administration*, Vol. 2, No. 3, July 1984, pp. 28-32.
32. McAvoy, L., & Dustin, D. "The Right to Risk in Wilderness." *Journal of Forestry*, Vol. 79, No. 3, March 1981, pp. 150-152.
33. McAvoy, L., & Dustin, D. "In Search of Balance: a No-Rescue Wilderness Proposal." *Western Wildlands*, Vol. 9, No. 2, Summer 1983, pp. 2-5.
34. McAvoy, L., & Dustin, D. "No One Will Come." *Backpacker*, Vol. 12, No. 5, September 1984, pp. 60-62, 64-65, 88.
35. McAvoy, L., Dustin, D., Rankin, J., & Frakt, A. "Wilderness and Legal Liability: Guidelines for Resource Managers and Program Leaders." *Journal of Park and Recreation Administration*, Vol. 3, No. 1, Winter 1985, pp. 41-49.
36. McAvoy, L., & Dustin, D. "Regulating Risks in the Nation's Parks." *Trends*, Vol. 22, No. 3, 1985, pp. 27-30.
37. Allen, S. "No-Rescue Wilderness—A Risky Proposition." *Journal of Forestry*, Vol. 79, No. 3, March 1981, pp. 153-154.
38. Peterson, D. "Look Ma, No Hands! Here's What's Wrong With No-Rescue Wilderness." Parks & Recreation, Vol. 22, No. 6, June 1987, pp. 39-43, 54.

Chapter 7 (Opportunities for Choice)

1. *Report of the National Advisory Commission on Civil Disorders.* New York, NY: Bantam Books, 1968.
2. Ibid, pp. 143-150.
3. Kraus, R. "Recreation and Civil Disorder." *Parks & Recreation*, Vol. III, No. 7, July 1968, pp. 38-39, 48-49.
4. Gray, D., & Greben, S. "Future Perspectives." *Parks & Recreation*, Vol. IX, No. 6, July 1974, pp. 26-33, 47-56.
5. Gray, D., & Greben, S. "Future Perspectives II: The 1980s and Beyond." *Parks & Recreation*, Vol. 17, No. 5, May 1982, pp. 52-56.

6. See Dustin, D., & Peterson, D. "Taking the Pulse of NRPA." *California Parks & Recreation*, Vol. 38, No. 2, April/ May 1982, pp. 21-23.

7. Clawson, M., & Knetsch, J. *Economics of Outdoor Recreation.* Baltimore, MD: The Johns Hopkins Press, 1966.

8. Ibid, p. 267.

9. Ibid.

10. See Driver, B., Brown, P., & Peterson, G. (Eds.) *Benefits of Leisure.* State College, PA: Venture Publishing, Inc., 1991, for a comprehensive discussion of the progress that has been made in verifying the benefits of parks and recreation.

11. See Parks and Recreation Federation of Ontario. *The Benefits of Parks and Recreation.* Gloucester, Ontario: Canadian Parks/ Recreation Association, 1993, for lists of benefits of leisure and accompanying research citations for each benefit.

12. Schultz, J., McAvoy, L., & Dustin, D. "What Are We in Business For?" *Parks & Recreation*, Vol. 23, No. 1, January 1988, pp. 52-54.

13. Dustin, D., McAvoy, L., & Schultz, J. "Beware of the Merchant Mentality." *Trends*, Vol. 24, No. 3, 1987, pp. 44-46.

14. Dustin, D. "Leisure: a Futurist's Perspective." *California Parks & Recreation*, Vol. 35, No. 3, August/September 1979, pp. 10-11.

15. Ibid, p. 11.

16. Ibid.

17. Dustin, D., McAvoy, L., & Beck, L. "Promoting Recreationist Self-Sufficiency." *Journal of Park and Recreation Administration*, Vol. 4, No. 4, Winter 1986, pp. 43-52.

18. Dustin, D., McAvoy, L., & Schultz, J. "Recreation Rightly Understood." In Goodale, T. and Witt, P. (Eds.) *Recreation and Leisure: Issues in an Era of Change.* 3rd edition. State College, PA: Venture Publishing, Inc., 1991, pp. 97-106.

19. Dustin, D., Knopf, R., & Fox, K. "Building Multicultural Responsiveness into Outdoor Recreation Management." In A. Ewert, D. Chavez, & A. Magill (Eds.) *Culture, Conflict and Communication at the Wildland/Urban Interface.* Boulder, CO: Westview Press, 1993, pp. 259-265.

20. Dustin, D. "Peace, Leisure and Recreation." *Parks & Recreation*, Vol. 26, No. 9, September 1991, pp. 102-104.

Chapter 8 (Breaking the Language Barrier)

1. Newman, E. *Strictly Speaking*. New York, N.Y.: Warner Books, 1974.
2. Adler, R., & Towne, N. *Looking Out/Looking In: Interpersonal Communication*. San Francisco, CA: Rinehart Press, 1975.
3. Rettie, D. "A New Perspective on Leisure." *Parks & Recreation*, Vol. IX, No. 8, August 1974, pp. 20-25, 41-46.
4. Ibid, pp. 24-25.
5. Adler & Towne, p. 279.
6. Whorf, B. *Language, Thought, and Reality*. Cambridge, MA: The M. I. T. Press, 1956.
7. Ibid, p. 213.
8. Condon, J. *Semantics and Communication*. New York, NY: The Macmillan Company, 1966.
9. Ibid, p. 31.
10. Ibid, p. 32.
11. Toffler, A. *Future Shock*. New York, NY: Bantam Books, 1970.
12. Condon, p. 55.
13. Rettie, p. 41.
14. Gray, D., & Greben, S. "Future Perspectives." *California Parks & Recreation*, Vol. 30, No. 3, June/July 1974, pp. 11-19.
15. Gray, D. "WANTED: A New Word for Recreation." *Parks & Recreation*, Vol. IX, No. 3, March 1974, p. 23.
16. Condon, p. 48.
17. Dustin, D. "Leisure: a Futurist's Perspective." *California Parks & Recreation*, Vol. 35, No. 3, August/September 1979, pp. 10-11.
18. Ibid, p. 11.
19. Condon, p. 49.
20. Ibid, p. 14.
21. Ibid.
22. Dustin, p. 11.
23. Bois, J. *The Art of Awareness*. Dubuque, IA: Wm. C. Brown Company, 1966.
24. Watts, A. *The Wisdom of Insecurity*. New York, NY: Pantheon, 1951.

Chapter 9 (Creating Natural Resources)

1. Brown, W. *Islands of Hope*. Arlington, VA: National Recreation and Park Association, 1971.
2. McAvoy, L. "An Environmental Ethic for Parks and Recreation." *Parks and Recreation, 25* (9), 1990, pp. 68-72.
3. Whorf, B. *Language, Thought, and Reality*. Cambridge, MA: The M. I. T. Press, 1956.
4. Ibid, p. vi.
5. Ibid.
6. Spoehr, A. "Cultural Differences in the Interpretation of Natural Resources." In William L. Thomas, Jr. (Ed.) *Man's Role in Changing the Face of the Earth*. Chicago, IL: University of Chicago Press, 1956, pp. 93-102.
7. Ibid, p. 93.
8. Ibid., p. 99.
9. Ibid.
10. Dustin, D. "Reifying Recreation Resources." In *Proceedings of the 3rd Annual Intermountain Leisure Symposium*. Provo, UT: Brigham Young University, November 1982, pp. 107-108.
11. Condon, J., Jr. *Semantics and Communication*. New York, NY: The Macmillan Company, 1966.
12. U. S. Public Law 88-577 in U. S., *Statutes at Large*. 78, pp. 890-96.
13. Nash, R. *Wilderness and the American Mind*. New Haven, CT: Yale University Press, 1967.
14. Merriam, L., & Knopp, T. "Meeting the Wilderness Needs of the Many." *Western Wildlands, 3*(2), 1976, pp. 17-22.
15. Leopold, A. *A Sand County Almanac*. New York, NY: Oxford University Press, 1949.
16. Lee, C. "Energy and its Impact on Leisure Services." Paper presented at the California and Pacific Southwest Park and Recreation Conference in San Diego, CA, March, 1981.
17. Spoehr, p. 95.
18. Jubenville, A. *Outdoor Recreation Planning*. Philadelphia, PA: W. B. Saunders Company, 1976.
19. Spoehr, p. 94.
20. Ibid, p.96.

21. Ibid., p. 97.
22. Dustin, D. "Recreational Usufruct Rights." In *Proceedings of the 4th Annual Intermountain Leisure Symposium*. Provo, UT: Brigham Young University, November 1983, pp. 25-26.
23. Olson, S. *Reflections from The North Country*. New York, NY: Alfred A. Knopf, 1977.
24. Spoehr, p. 99.
25. Ibid, p. 97.
26. Ibid, p. 100.
27. Bronowski, J. *Science and Human Values*. New York, NY: Harper Colophon Books,1975, p. 119.
28. Bois, J. *The Art Of Awareness*. Dubuque, IA: Wm. C. Brown Company Publishers, 1966.
29. Stone, C. *Should Trees Have Standing?* Los Altos, CA: William Kaufmann, Inc., 1974.
30. Johnson, W. *Muddling Toward Frugality*. Boulder, CO: Shambhala, 1979.
31. Hardin, G. "Rewards of Pejoristic Thinking." In *Managing the Commons*. San Francisco, CA: W. H. Freeman and Company, 1977.
32. Reiser, O. *Cosmic Humanism*. Cambridge, MA: Schenkman Publishing Company, 1966.
33. Schumacher, E. *Small is Beautiful: Economics as if People Mattered*. New York, NY: Harper & Row Publishers, 1973.
34. Reiser, O. *Cosmic Humanism and World Unity*. New York, NY: Gordon and Breach, Science Publishers, Inc., 1975.
35. Ibid, p. 18.
36. Ibid.
37. Whorf, p. 263.
38. Schumacher, pp. 138-151.
39. Johnson, pp. 97-100.
40. Mesthene, E. "How Technology Will Shape the Future." In *Purposive Systems*. New York, NY: Spartan Books, 1968, pp. 67-77.
41. Laszlo, E. *The Systems View of The World*. New York, NY: George Braziller, 1972.
42. Mitchell, A. *Changing Values and Lifestyles*. Menlo Park, CA: SRI International, 1980.

43. See Nash, R. *The Rights of Nature: A History of Environmental Ethics.* Madison, WI: University of Wisconsin Press, 1989.
44. Leopold, p. 209.
45. U. S. Public law 91-190, Section 2.
46. Laszlo, p. 47.
47. Storm, H. "Eolithism and Design." *Colorado Quarterly*, 1, (3), Winter, 1953.
48. Dustin, D., & McAvoy, L. "Toward Environmental Eolithism." *Environmental Ethics*, Vol. 6, No. 2, Summer 1984, pp. 161-166.
49. Hawkins, D. "The Nature of Purpose." In *Purposive Systems.* New York, NY: Spartan Books, 1968, pp. 163-179.
50. Ibid, p. 170.
51. Laszlo, p. 10.
52. Hawkins, p. 166.
53. Ibid, p. 165.
54. Olson, p. 59.

Chapter 10 (Reaching for a Higher Education)

1. Clark, J. "The General Ecology of Knowledge in Curriculums of the Future." In E. Laszlo (Ed.) *The Relevance of General Systems Theory.* New York, NY: George Braziller, 1972, pp. 163-180.
2. Sessoms, H. "Our Body of Knowledge; Myth or Reality?" *Parks & Recreation*, Vol. 10, No. 11, November, 1975, pp. 30-31, 38.
3. Mead, B. "Recreation Semantics 101." *Parks & Recreation*, Vol. 12, No. 10, October, 1977, pp. 26-28, 44-45.
4. Henkel, D. ". . . Professionalism." *Parks & Recreation*, Vol. 22, No. 7, July 1976, pp. 52-53.
5. See the 1991 issue of *Schole: A Journal of Leisure Studies and Recreation Education* for a discussion of the pros and cons of accreditation of park and recreation programs in higher education.
6. Albert, R., "Professionalism and Educational Reform." *The Journal of Higher Education*, Vol. 51, No. 5, September/October 1980, pp. 497-518.

7. Laszlo, E. *The Systems View of the World.* New York, NY: George Braziller, 1972.
8. Nash, R. "Logs, Universities and the Environmental Education Compromise." *The Journal of Environmental Education*, Vol. 8, No. 2, Winter 1976, pp. 2-11.
9. Laszlo, p. 4.
10. Ibid, p. 5.
11. Mead, B. "Recreation Education: A Call for Change." *Parks & Recreation*, Vol. 14, No. 12, December 1979, pp. 38-39, 65.
12. Ibid, p. 38.
13. Laszlo, p. 3.
14. Geba, B. "The Roots of Recreation." *California Parks & Recreation*, Vol. 34, No. 3, August/September 1978, p. 6.
15. Nash, p. 8.
16. Sessoms, p. 31.
17. Driver, B. L. "Potential Contributions of Psychology to Recreation Resource Management." In Joachim Wohlwill and Daniel Carson (Eds.) *Environment and the Social Sciences; Perspectives and Applications.* Washington, DC: American Psychological Association, Inc., 1972, pp. 233-244.
18. Drucker, P. *The Age of Discontinuity*, New York, NY: Harper & Row, 1969.
19. Clark, J. "Systems Philosophy and the Crisis of Fragmentation in Education," In E. Laszlo (Ed.), *Introduction to Systems Philosophy.* New York, NY: Gordon and Breach Science Publishers, 1972, pp. 301-310.
20. Ibid.
21. See Bertalanffy, L. *General Systems Theory.* New York, NY: George Braziller, 1968.
22. See Schultz, J. "Trends in Education." *Parks & Recreation*, Vol. 16, No. 2, February 1980, pp. 71-74.
23. Laszlo, p. 21.
24. Crompton, J. "A Recreation System Model." *Leisure Sciences*, Vol. 1, No. 1, 1977, pp. 53-65.
25. See Livesey, L., Jr. "Noetic Planning: The Need to Know, But What?" In E. Laszlo (Ed.), *The Relevance of General Systems Theory.* New York NY: George Braziller, 1972, pp. 145-162.
26. Clark, "Systems Philosophy and the Crisis of Fragmentation in Education," p. 309.

27. Mead, "Recreation Education: A Call for Change," p. 65.
28. Clark, "The General Ecology of Knowledge in Curriculums of the Future," p. 171.
29. Boulding, K. "General Systems Theory: The Skeleton of Science." *Management Science*, Vol. 2, No. 3, April 1956, pp. 197-208.
30. Nash, p. 8.
31. Bruner, J. *Toward a Theory of Instruction*. Cambridge, MA: The Belkings Press of Harvard University Press, 1966.
32. Driver, B. "Introduction to the Basic Concepts of General Systems Theory." Unpublished Paper. University of Michigan, 1973.

Chapter 11 (Serving the Human Potential)

1. Maslow, A. *Motivation and Personality*. New York, NY: Harper & Row, 1954.
2. Laszlo, E. *The Systems View of the World*. New York, NY: George Braziller, 1972.
3. Based on an address delivered by Dr. Paul Saltman of the University of California at San Diego to delegates of the California and Pacific Southwest Park and Recreation Conference in San Diego, California, in March 1981.
4. Hayflick, L. "Cytogerontology." In Rockstein, M., Sussman, M., and Chesky, J. (Eds.), *Theoretical aspects of aging*, 1974, pp. 83- 103.
5. Siegel, R. "Genetics of aging and the life cycle in ciliates." *Proceedings of the Society of Experimental Biology*, Vol. 21, 1967, pp.127-148.
6. Hayflick, L. "Cell Aging." In Cherkin, A., et al. (Eds.), *Physiology and Cell Biology of Aging*. Aging Series (Vol. 8), New York, NY: Raven Press, 1979, pp. 3-19.
7. See Dubos, R. "Adaptation and Its Dangers." In *Man Adapting*. New Haven, CT: Yale University Press, 1965, pp. 254-279.
8. Hawkins, D. "The Nature of Purpose." In *Purposive Systems*. New York, NY: Spartan Books, 1968, pp. 163-179.
9. Ibid.

10. Based on an address delivered by Dr. Arthur Harkins of the University of Minnesota to students and faculty of San Diego State University in April 1979.
11. Laszlo, p. 110.
12. Ibid, p. 72.
13. See Dustin, D. "The Dance of the Dispossessed: On Patriarchy, Feminism and the Practice of Leisure Science." *Journal of Leisure Research*, Vol. 24, No. 4., 1992, pp. 324-332.
14. See Fox, K. "Choreographing Differences in the Dance of Leisure: The Potential of Feminist Thought." *Journal of Leisure Research*, Vol. 24, No. 4, 1992, pp. 333-347.
15. From the J. B. Nash Scholar Lecture by Dr. Karla Henderson at the 1993 AAHPERD convention.
16. Laszlo, p. 115.
17. Dustin, D., McAvoy, L., & Beck, L. "Promoting Recreationist Self-Sufficiency." *Journal of Park and Recreation Administration*, Vol. 4, No. 4, Winter 1986, pp. 43-52.
18. Sagoff, M. "The Philosopher as Teacher: On Teaching Environmental Ethics." *Metaphilosophy*, Vol. 11, Nos. 3 & 4, July/October, 1980, pp. 307-325.
19. See McAvoy, L., & Dustin, D. "The Right to Risk in Wilderness." *Journal of Forestry*, Vol. 79, No. 3, March 1981, pp. 150-152.
20. Sagoff, p. 319.
21. Dustin, D. "To Feed or Not Feed the Bears: The Moral Choices We Make." *Parks & Recreation*, Vol. 20, No. 10, October 1985, pp. 54-57, 72.
22. Leopold, A. *A Sand County Almanac.* New York, NY: Oxford University Press, 1949.
23. Laszlo, p. 75.

Chapter 12 (Rethinking Recreation and Leisure in Contemporary Life: An Ecopsychological Perspective)

1. Hillman, J. "A Psyche the Size of the Earth." In T. Roszak, M. Gomes, & A. Kanner (Eds.), *Ecopsychology: Restoring the Earth/Healing the Mind.* San Francisco, CA: Sierra Club Books, 1995, p. xvii.
2. Watts, A. *Psychotherapy, East and West.* New York, NY: Vintage Books, 1975.

3. Hardin, G. "The Tragedy of the Commons." *Science*, 162, December 13, 1968, pp. 1243-1248.
4. Rolston, H. "Nature, Spirit, and Landscape Management." In B. Driver, D. Dustin, T. Baltic, G. Elsner, & G. Peterson (Eds.), *Nature and the Human Spirit: Toward an Expanded Land Management Ethic.* State College, PA: Venture Publishing, Inc., 1996, pp. 17-24.
5. Bateson, G. *Mind and Nature.* New York, NY: Dutton, 1979.
6. James, W. *Talks to Teachers on Psychology.* New York, NY: Henry Holt, 1899.
7. Leopold, A. *A Sand County Almanac.* New York, NY: Oxford University Press, 1949.
8. Bronowski, J. *Science and Human Values* (2nd ed.). New York, NY: Harper & Row Publishers, 1965.
9. Bronowski, J. *The Identity of Man* (revised ed.). Garden City, NY: The Doubleday/Natural History Press, 1971, p. 19.
10. Ibid.
11. Boulding, K. "Commons and Community: The Idea of a Public." In G. Hardin and J. Baden (Eds.), *Managing the Commons.* San Francisco, CA: W. H. Freeman and Company, 1977, p. 286.
12. Loc. Cit., p. 288.
13. Kohlberg, L. *The Psychology of Moral Development: The Nature and Validity of Moral Stages.* San Francisco, CA: Harper & Row, 1984.
14. Gilligan, C. *In a Different Voice.* Cambridge, MA: Harvard University Press, 1982.
15. Leopold, 1949.
16. Schweitzer, A. *The Teaching of Reverence for Life.* New York, NY: Holt, Rinehart and Winston, 1965.
17. Oelschlaeger, M. *The Idea of Wilderness.* New Haven, CT: Yale University Press, 1991.
18. Nash, R. *The Rights of Nature: A History of Environmental Ethics.* Madison, WI: The University of Wisconsin Press, 1989.
19. Shepard, P. "Where Psyche Meets Gaia." In T. Roszak, M. Gomes, & A. Kanner (Eds.), *Ecopsychology: Restoring the Earth/Healing the Mind.* San Francisco, CA: Sierra Club Books, 1995, p. 13.

20. Roberts, E. "Place and Spirit in Landscape Management." In B. Driver, D. Dustin, T. Baltic, G. Elsner, & G. Peterson (Eds.), *Nature and the Human Spirit: Toward an Expanded Land Management Ethic.* State College, PA: Venture Publishing, Inc., 1996, pp. 61-80.
21. Macy, J. *World as Lover, World as Self.* Berkeley, CA: Parallax Press, 1993.
22. Lovelock, J. *Gaia: A New Look at Life on earth.* New York, NY: Oxford University Press, 1979.
23. Wilson, E., & Kellert, S. *The Biophilia Hypothesis.* Washington, D.C.: Island Press/Shearwater Books, 1993.
24. Dustin, D., McAvoy, L., & Goodale, T. "The Benefits Equation." *Parks & Recreation, 34,* 1, 1999, p. 32.
25. Dustin, D., & Goodale, T. "The Social Costs of Individual 'Benefits.'" *Parks & Recreation, 32,* 7, 1997, pp. 20-22.
26. Ornstein, R., & Sobel, D. *Healthy Pleasures.* Reading, MA: Addison-Wesley Publishing Co., Inc., 1989, p. 22.
27. Ibid.
28. Dustin et al., 1999.
29. Hillman, 1995, p. xviii.
30. Loc. cit., p. xx.
31. Olson, S. *Reflections from the North Country.* New York, NY: Alfred A. Knopf, 1997, p. 59.
32. Freud, S. *Civilization and its Discontents* (translated by James Strachey). New York, NY: Norton, 1961, p. 13.
33. Roszak, 1995, p. 17.
34. Thoreau, H. *Walden.* Boston, MA: Tichnor and Fields, 1854, p. 297.

Chapter 13 (People and Nature: Toward an Ecological Model of Health Promotion)

1. Louv, R. *Last Child in the Woods: Saving Our Children from Nature-Deficit Disorder.* Chapel Hill, NC: Algonquin Books, 2005.

2. U.S. Department of Health and Human Services. "Overweight and obesity: Health consequences." Atlanta, GA: U. S. Department of Health and Human Services, Centers for Disease Control and Prevention. Retrieved December 13, 2008, from http://www.cdc.gov/nccdphp/dnpa/obesity/consequences.htm.

3. Clements, R. "An investigation of the state of outdoor play." Contemporary Issues in *Early Childhood, 5*(1), 2004, pp. 68-80.

4. Kellert, S. *Building for Life: Designing and Understanding the Human-Nature Connection.* Washington, DC: Island Press, 2005.

5. Outdoor Industry Foundation. Outdoor Recreation Participation Study for 2008. Retrieved February 10, 2009, from http://www.outdoorfoundation.org/research.participation.2008.html.

6. Pergams, O., & Zaradic, P. "Is love of nature in the US becoming love of electronic media? 16-year downtrend in national park visits explained by watching movies, playing video games, internet use, and oil prices." *Journal of Environmental Management, 80*(4), 2006, pp. 287-293.

7. Turner, W., Nakamura, T., & Dinetti, M. "Global urbanization and the separation of humans from nature." *BioScience, 54*(6), 2004, pp. 585-590.

8. Faber Taylor, A., & Kuo, F. "Is contact with nature important for healthy child development? State of the evidence." In C. Spencer & M. Blades (Eds.), *Children and Their Environments: Learning, Using and Designing Spaces.* Cambridge, UK: Cambridge University Press, 2006, pp. 124-158.

9. Faber Taylor, A., Kuo, F., & Sullivan, W. "Views of nature and self-discipline: Evidence from inner city children." *Journal of Environmental Psychology, 22*, 2002, pp. 49-63.

10. Kellert, 2005.

11. Chawla, L. "Significant life experiences revisited: a review of research on sources of environmental sensitivity." *Journal of Environmental Education, 29*(3), 1998, pp. 11-21.

12. Chawla, L. "Children's concern for the natural environment." *Children's Environments Quarterly, 5*(3), 1988, pp. 13-20.

13. Kaplan, R., & Kaplan, S. *The Experience of Nature: A Psychological Perspective.* Cambridge, UK: Cambridge University Press, 1989.

14. Wilson, E. "Biophilia and the conservation ethic." In S. Kellert & E. Wilson (Eds.), *The Biophilia Hypothesis.* Washington, DC: Island Press, 1993, pp. 31-41.
15. Altman, I., & Wohlwill, J. (Eds.). *Human Behavior and Environment: Advances in Theory and Research.* New York: Plenum Press, 1983.
16. Chivian, E., & Bernstein, A. (Eds.) *Sustaining life: How Human Health Depends on Biodiversity.* New York: Oxford University Press, 2008.
17. Kellert, 2005.
18. Kaplan, R. & Kaplan, S., 1989.
19. Proshansky, H., Ittelson, W., & Rivlin, L. (Eds.) *Environmental Psychology: Man and His Physical Setting.* New York: Holt, Rinehart and Winston, 1970.
20. U.S. Bureau of Labor Statistics. Retrieved February 10, 2009, from http://www.bls.gov/tus/datafiles_2006.htm.
21. Kaiser Foundation. Generation M: Media in the lives of 8-18 year-olds. Retrieved March 2, 2009, from www.kff.org/entmedia/7250.cfm.
22. Robinson, J., & Godbey, G. *Time for Life: The Surprising Ways Americans Use Their Time.* University Park, PA: The Pennsylvania State University Press, 1997.
23. National Alliance for Nutrition and Activity. Obesity and other diet and inactivity-related diseases: National impact, costs, and solutions. Retrieved March 17, 2009, from www.cspinet.org/nutritionpolicy/briefingbookfy04.ppt.
24. American Institute of Stress. America's no. 1 health problem. Retrieved March 5, 2009, from http://www.stress.org/about.htm.
25. Giles-Corti, B., & Donovan R. Relative influences of individual, social environmental, and physical environmental correlates of walking. *American Journal of Public Health, 93*, 2003, pp. 1583-1589.
26. Gobster, P. "Neighborhood open space relationships in metropolitan planning: A look across four scales of concern." *Local Environment, 6*, 2001, pp. 199-212.

27. Sasidharan, V., Willits, F., & Godbey, G. "Cultural differences in urban recreation patterns: an examination of park usage and activity participation across six population subgroups." *Managing Leisure, 10*, 2005, pp. 19-38.
28. Godbey, G. *Outdoor Recreation and Health: Understanding and Enhancing the Relation.* Washington, DC: Resources for the Future, 2009.
29. Kaczynski, A., & Henderson, K. "Environmental correlates of physical activity: A review of evidence about parks and recreation." *Leisure Sciences, 29*(4), 2007, pp. 315-354.
30. Kaczynski A., Potwarka L., & Saelens, B. "Association of park size, distance, and features with physical activity in neighborhood parks." *American Journal of Public Health, 98*(8), 2008, pp. 1451-1456.
31. Kahn, E., Ramsey, L., Brownson, R., Heath, G., Howze, E., Powell, K., et al. "The   effectiveness of interventions to increase physical activity." *American Journal of Preventive Medicine, 22*(4S), 2002, pp. 87-88.
32. Sallis, J., Prochaska, J., & Taylor, W. "A Review of Correlates of Physical Activity of Children and Adolescents." *Medicine and Science in Sports and Exercise, 32*, 2000, pp. 963-975.
33. Frumkin, H. "Healthy places: Exploring the evidence." *American Journal of Public Health, 93*(9), 2003, pp. 1451-1456.
34. Kaplan, S. "The restorative benefits of nature: Toward an integrative framework." *Journal of Environmental Psychology, 15*, 1995, pp. 169-182.
35. Ulrich, R. "Natural versus urban scenes: Some psychophysiological effects." *Environment and Behavior, 13*(5), 1981, pp. 523-556.
36. Payne, L., Orsega-Smith, E., Roy, M., & Godbey, G. "Local park use and personal health among older adults: An exploratory study." *Journal of Park and Recreation Administration, 23*(2), 2005, pp. 1-20.
37. Godbey, 2009.
38. Chase D., & Godbey, G. "The accuracy of self-reported participation rates: A research note." *Leisure Studies, 2*, 1983, pp. 123-126.

39. Chase, D., & Harada, H. "Response error in self-reported recreation participation." *Journal of Leisure Research, 16* (4), 1994, pp. 322-329.
40. Godbey, 2009.
41. Sallis, Prochaska, & Taylor, 2000.
42. Bixler, R., & Floyd, M. "Nature is scary, disgusting and uncomfortable." *Environment and Behavior, 29*, 1997, pp. 443-467.
43. Floyd, M., Spengler, J., Maddock, J., Gobster, P., & Suau, L. "Park-based physical activity in diverse communities of two U. S. cities: An observational study." *American Journal of Preventive Medicine, 34*, 2008, pp. 299-305.
44. Louv, 2005.
45. Green Hour. Retrieved March 28, 2009, from http://www.greenhour.org.
46. Godbey, 2009.
47. Ibid.
48. Chow, H. *Physically Active Leisure Among Older Adults— Measurement, Comparison and Impact.* Saarbrucken, Germany: VDM Verlag Publishers, 2007.
49. Godbey, 2009.
50. Hartig, T., & Evans, G. "Psychological foundation of nature experience." In T. Garling & R. Golledge (Eds.), *Behavior and Environment: Psychological and Geographical Approaches.* Bridgewater, NJ: Elsevier Science, 1993.
51. Kweon, B., Ellis, C., Lee, S., & Rogers, G. "Large-scale environmental knowledge: Investigating the relationship between self-reported and objectively measured physical environments." *Environment and Behavior, 38*(1), 2006, pp. 72-91.
52. Ulrich, R. "Aesthetic and affective response to natural environment." In I. Altman & J. Wohlwill (Eds.), *Human Behavior and Environment: Advances in Theory and Research.* New York: Plenum Press, 1983.
53. Hartig & Evans, 1993.
54. Hartig, T., Mang, M., & Evans, G. "Restorative effects of natural environment experiences." *Environment and Behavior, 23*(1), 1991, pp. 3-26.

55. Rybczynski, W. *A Clearing in the Distance: Frederick Law Olmsted and America in the Nineteenth Century.* New York: Scribner, 1999.
56. Sax, J. *Mountains without Handrails: Reflections on the National Parks.* Ann Arbor, MI: The University of Michigan Press, 1980.
57. Godbey, 2009.
58. American Forests. Projected environmental benefits of community tree planting: A multi-site urban forest project in Atlanta. Washington, DC: American Forests. Retrieved February 2, 2009, from http://www.americanforests.org/downloads/rea/AF_Atlanta2.pdf.
59. Center for Urban Horticulture, University of Washington. Retrieved March 15, 2009, from http://www.cfr.washington.edu/Research/fact_sheets/20-UrbEconBen.pdf.
60. Rail to Trails Conservancy. Retrieved May 3, 2009, from http://www.railstotrails.org/whatwedo/railtrailinfo/benefits.html.
61. Takano, T., Nakamura, K., & Watanabe, T. "Urban residential environments and senior citizens' longevity in megacity areas: The importance of walkable green spaces." *Journal of Epidemiology and Community Health, 56*(12), 2002, pp. 913-918.
62. S. Kaplan, 1995.
63. Bodin, M., & Hartig, T. "Does the outdoor environment matter for psychological restoration gained through running?" *Psychology of Sport Exercise, 4*(2), 2003, pp. 142-153.
64. Faber Taylor, A., Kuo, F., & Sullivan, W. "Coping with ADD: The surprising connection to green play settings." *Environment and Behavior, 33*(1), 2001, pp. 54-77.
65. Kuo, F., & Faber Taylor, A. "A potential natural treatment for Attention-Deficit/Hyperactivity Disorder: Evidence from a national study." *American Journal of Public Health, 94*(9), 2004, pp. 1580-1586.
66. Kaplan, R. "The nature of the view from home: Psychological benefits." *Environment and Behavior, 33*(4), 1991, pp. 507-542.
67. Ulrich, R. "View through a window may influence recovery from surgery." *Science*, 224, 1984, pp. 420-421.

68. Beatley, T. *Green Urbanism: Learning from European Cities.* Washington, DC: Island Press, 2000.
69. Robert Wood Johnson Foundation. *Healthy Places, Healthy People: Promoting Public Health and Physical Activity Through Community Design.* Princeton, NJ: Robert Wood Johnson, 2000.
70. Schwab, K., Dustin, D., & Bricker, K. "Parks, recreation and tourism's contributions to Utah's health: An ecologic perspective." *Leisure Insights, 29*(1), 2009, pp. 12-14.
71. Chivian, E. "Beyond wildlife-health and conservation." In D. Roe, (Ed.), *The Millennium Development Goals and Conservation: Managing Nature's Wealth for Society's Health.* London: International Institute for Environment and Development, 2004, pp. 26-27.
72. Millennium Ecosystem Assessment. *Ecosystems and Human well-being: A Framework for Assessment.* Washington, DC: Island Press, 2003.
73. Chivian, 2004.
74. Chivian, E., & Bernstein, A. (Guest Editorial): "Embedded in nature: Human health and biodiversity." *Environmental Health Perspectives, 112*(1), 2004, A12-A13.
75. Chivian, 2004.
76. Annan, K. Prologue. In E. Chivian, & A. Bernstein (Eds.), *Sustaining Life: How Human Health Depends on Biodiversity.* New York: Oxford University Press, ix, 2008.
77. Pretty, J., Peacock, J., Sellens, M., & Griffin, M. "The mental and physical health outcomes of green exercise." *International Journal of Environmental Health Research, 15*(5), 2005, pp. 319-337.
78. Van den Berg, A., Hartig, T., & Staats, H. "Preference for nature in urbanized societies: Stress, restoration, and the pursuit of sustainability." *Journal of Social Issues, 63*(1), 2007, pp. 79-96.
79. Dustin, D., & McAvoy, L. "The Decline and fall of quality recreation opportunities and environments?" *Environmental Ethics, 4*(1), 1982, pp. 49-57.
80. Godbey, 2009.

81. Hancock, T. Healthy and sustainable communities—creating community capital. In: 4th European IUHPE Conference on Effectiveness and Quality of Health Promotion. *IUHPE*, 16-19 May, 1999, Tallinn, Estonia.

82. Chu, C., & Simpson, R. *Ecological Public Health: From Vision to Practice.* Institute of Applied Environmental Research, Griffith University, Queensland, Australia and Centre for Health Promotion, University of Toronto, Canada, 1994.

83. Maller, C., Townsend, M., Pryor, A., Brown, P., & St. Leger, L. "Healthy nature healthy people: 'Contact with Nature' as an upstream health promotion intervention for populations." *Health Promotion International, 21*, 2006, pp. 45-54.

84. Floyd, M., Crespo, C., & Sallis, J. "Active living in diverse and disadvantaged communities: Stimulating dialogue and policy solutions." *American Journal of Preventive Medicine, 34*, 2008, pp. 271-274.

85. Shinew, K., Stodolska, M., Floyd, M., Hibbler, D., Allison, M., Johnson, C., et al. "Race and ethnicity in leisure behavior: Where have we been and where do we need to go." *Leisure Sciences, 28*, 2006, pp. 403-408.

86. Floyd, M., & Johnson, C. "Coming to terms with environmental justice in outdoor recreation: A conceptual discussion with research implications." *Leisure Sciences, 24*, 2002, pp. 59-77.

87. U.S. Census Bureau. Retrieved January 25, 2009, from http://www.census.gov/population/www/socdemo/age/age_2006.html.

88. Spangler, K., & Caldwell, L. "The implications of public policy related to parks, recreation, and public health: A focus on physical activity." *Journal of Physical Activity and Health, 4*(1), 2007, pp. 64-71.

89. Driver, B. (Ed.). *Managing to Optimize the Beneficial Outcomes of Recreation.* State College, PA: Venture Publishing, 2009.

90. Godbey, G., Caldwell, L., Floyd, M., & Payne, L. "Contributions of leisure studies and recreation and park management research to the active living agenda." *American Journal of Preventive Medicine, 28* (2), 2005, pp. 150-158.

91. Brandon, K. Ecotourism and conservation: A review of key issues. *Environmental Department Papers* (No. 033). Washington, DC: The World Bank, 1996.
92. McAvoy, L., Dustin, D., & Clements, C. "Tourism's role in building a better world." In J. Zeiger and L. Caneday (Eds.), *Tourism and Leisure: Dynamics and Diversity* (pp. 93-102). Alexandria, VA: NRPA, 1991.
93. Dustin, D., McAvoy, L., & Goodale, T. "The benefits equation." *Parks & Recreation, 34*(1), 1999, pp. 32-37.
94. Dustin, D. "The Dance of the dispossessed: On patriarchy, feminism, and the practice of leisure science." *Journal of Leisure Research, 24*(4), 1992, pp. 324-332.
95. Rolston, H. "Nature, spirit, and landscape management." In B. Driver, D. Dustin, T. Baltic, G. Elsner, & G. Peterson (Eds.), *Nature and the Human Spirit: Toward an Expanded Land Management Ethic.* State College, PA: Venture Publishing, Inc., 1996, pp. 17-24.
96. Dustin, D. "The weight of the world: Why camp is ever more important." *Camping Magazine, 66*(4), 1994, p. 31.

Chapter 14 (Ecological Democracy: Cultivating Healthy Citizens)

1. Dustin, D. "Recreational Ethics in a World of Limits." *Parks & Recreation, 19* (3), 1984, pp. 48-51, 70.
2. For a practical illustration of this symbiotic relationship see Dustin, D., Schwab, K., & Bricker, K. "Thermus Aquaticus and You: Biodiversity, Human Health, and the Interpretive Challenge." *Rural Connections*, September 2010, pp. 47-50.
3. Hardin, G. "The Tragedy of the Commons." *Science*, 162, December 13, 1968, pp. 1243-1248.
4. Boulding, K. "Commons and Community: The Idea of a Public." In Hardin, G. and Baden, J. (Eds.), *Managing the Commons.* San Francisco, CA: W. H. Freeman and Company, 1977, pp. 280-294.

5. McAfee, K., & Shapiro, E. "Payments for ecosystem services in Mexico: Nature, neoliberalism, social movements, and the state." *Annals of the Association of American Geographers, 100*(3), 2010, p. 595.
6. Shiva, V. *Earth Democracy.* Cambridge, MA: South End Press, 2006.
7. Ibid, p. 54.
8. Paisley, K. & Dustin, D. (Eds.). *Speaking Up and Speaking Out: Working for Social and Environmental Justice through Parks, Recreation, and Leisure.* Champaign, IL: Sagamore Publishing, LLC, 2011.
9. Sandel, M. Justice: *What's the right thing to do?* New York: Farrar, Straus & Giroux, 2009.
10. Loc cit., p. 265.
11. Loc cit., p.267.
12. Chase, S. (Ed.) *Defending the Earth: A Dialogue between Murray Bookchin and Dave Foreman.* Boston, MA: Southend Press, 1991, p. 131.
13. Glover, T. "Where Does Growth for Growth's Sake Lead Us?" In Paisley, K., & Dustin, D. (Eds.), *Speaking Up and Speaking Out: Working for Social and Environmental Justice through Parks, Recreation, and Leisure.* Champaign, IL: Sagamore Publishing, LLC, 2011, pp. 105-116.
14. Slater, P. *The Pursuit of Loneliness.* Boston, MA: Beacon Press, 1970.
15. Roe, D. (Ed.). *The Millennium Development Goals and Conservation: Managing Nature's Wealth for Society's Health.* London: International Institute for Environment and Development, 2004.
16. Orr, D. *Earth in Mind: On Education, Environment, and the Human Prospect.* Washington D.C.: Island Press, 2004, p. 170.
17. Smith, I. *Happy: Simple Steps to Get the Most Out of Life.* New York, NY: St. Martin's Press, 2010.
18. Hardin, 1968.
19. Kohlberg, L. *The Psychology of Moral Development: The Nature and Validity of Moral Stages.* San Francisco, CA: Harper & Row, 1984.

20. Gilligan, C. *In a Different Voice*. Cambridge, MA: Harvard University Press, 1982.
21. Dustin, D. "Back in the U.S.S.R." In *The Wilderness Within: Reflections on Leisure and Life*, 3rd edition. Champaign, IL: Sagamore Publishing, LLC, 2006, p. 85.
22. Dustin, D., & Goodale, T. "Reflections on Recreation, Park, and Leisure Studies." In E. Jackson & T. Burton (Eds.), *Leisure Studies: Prospects for the Twenty-First Century*. State College, PA: Venture Publishing, Inc., 1999, pp. 477-486.
23. Wellman, D., Dustin, D., Henderson, K., & Moore, R. *Service Living: Building Community Through Public Parks and Recreation*. State College, PA: Venture Publishing, Inc., 2008.